:: **The New Americans** ::

:: The New Americans ::

SEVEN FAMILIES JOURNEY TO
ANOTHER COUNTRY

Rubén Martínez

Photographs by Joseph Rodríguez

THE NEW PRESS

NEW YORK
LONDON

Published in the United States by The New Press, New York, 2004
Distributed by W. W. Norton & Company, Inc., New York

ISBN 1-56584-792-X (hc)
ISBN 1-56584-998-1 (pbk)
CIP data available

The New Press was established in 1990 as a not-for-profit alternative to the large,
commercial publishing houses currently dominating the book publishing industry. The
New Press operates in the public interest rather than for private gain, and is
committed to publishing, in innovative ways, works of educational, cultural, and
community value that are often deemed insufficiently profitable.

www.thenewpress.com

Book design by hot water

Printed in the United States of America

10   9   8   7   6   5   4   3   2   1

:: Contents ::

:: Acknowledgments ::

I owe a debt of gratitude to the filmmakers behind *The New Americans*, namely Steve James, Gordon Quinn, Jerry Blumenthal, Gita Saedi, Susanna Aiken, Carlos Aparicio, Fenell Dormeus, Indu Krishnan, Evangeline Griego, and Renée Tajima-Peña.

Susan Bergholz, my agent, was ever vigilant and diligent in watching my back.

Joe Rodríguez, as always, helped me to see.

It was a pleasure to work with my editor at The New Press, Andy Hsiao, whose own expertise on migration matters was of invaluable support. Thanks also to Steve Theodore and the rest of the crew at TNP.

Much of the research and some of the writing for this project occurred during my year as a Loeb Fellow at Harvard University's Graduate School of Design. A salute to my fellow fellows, and especially to Jim Stockard and Sally Young, for their generous hospitality.

The Lannan Foundation provided me with a generous fellowship as well, and made it possible for me to commune with several of my literary heroes and heroines, whose work on many of the themes in this book precedes mine: Luis Alberto Urrea, Denise Chávez, Benjamin Alire Saenz, and Demetria Martínez.

A loving embrace to my partner, Angela García, for helping me brave the stacks at Widener and exploring the big ideas with me.

To my friends and colleagues, my thanks for their editorial advice and moral support: Roberto Lovato, Ofelia Cuevas, Randy Williams, David Reid, Jayne Walker, Richard Rodríguez, Sandy Close, Marcelo Suárez-Orozco, Betto Arcos, Elijah Wald, Peggy Levitt, Carolina González, Omar Dewachi, and Hosam Aboul-Ela.

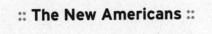

:: The New Americans ::

:: Prologue ::

Nativism as a habit of mind illuminates darkly some of the large contours of the American past; it has mirrored our national anxieties and marked out the bounds of our tolerance.

—John Higham, *Strangers in the Land*

::

IT WAS THE FRIDAY AFTER 9/11, AND I FOUND MYSELF ON A SMALL ISLAND OFF the coast of Maine. The occasion was an annual academic retreat. Our accommodations consisted of old army barracks turned, bizarrely, into time-share condos, but the hint of Great Diamond Island's military history did not diminish the physical beauty of the place. Still, the bucolic environs were unsettling, given the uncertain and frightening times. Emerging into the cool morning with a hint of autumn in the air, I was approached by two casually dressed men. I thought perhaps they were tourists, like me. Then they showed me their Bureau of Alcohol, Tobacco and Firearms badges.

It was certainly not the first time I'd been interrogated by federal authorities. I've had many such encounters, at airports and border crossings. I've been strip-searched in Nogales, Arizona, and detained at Los Angeles International Airport as a suspected drug trafficker (the officer even produced "evidence" supposedly found in my baggage). I've been told that there are many Rubén Martínezes in America, and that a few of them have serious criminal records; I've even been told to consider changing my name. (Do they mean consider changing the color of my skin?)

But that morning after 9/11 upped the ante considerably. The ATF agents said that a tip had been phoned in by an island resident about a group of "suspicious-acting foreign types." At the time, there were rumors that some of the hijackers had crossed into the States from Canada, and we all knew for certain that Mohammed Atta and at least one accomplice had been in the area prior to boarding American Airlines flight 11 at Logan Airport in Boston.

Apparently, I fit the description of a terrorist: dark skin and eyes, beard and moustache. What had been a hip "goatee" on 9/10 now denoted a possible threat to national security.

"Are you Middle Eastern?" one of the agents asked.

I explained that I was an American of Salvadoran and Mexican descent, and they asked me to show identification. After a few more questions, the agents seemed to become distracted. Another worthless tip, more time wasted. After some amicable banter (one of the agents was a former marine and a veteran of the Panama invasion of 1989; we chatted in Spanish), they apologized and bid me a good day. As an after-thought, I asked them whether I did indeed "look Middle Eastern."

"Honestly, yeah," one said.

"Might want to lose the facial hair," said the other.

I shaved that night, though several months later it crept back.

A year and half later, five days after the beginning of the second Gulf War, I read in the papers that the FBI had posted a worldwide alert for one Adnan G. El Shukrijumah, a Saudi national suspected of plotting terror attacks as part of al Qaeda. Shukrijumah was described as "about five-foot-four and one hundred thirty-two pounds, black hair, black eyes, with a Mediterranean complexion and possibly wearing a beard."

The FBI's description fit about 90 percent of Mexican and Central American males. Maybe it's time to shave again.

On the domestic front of the War on Terror, the FBI has fielded thousands of agents across the country to interview some 10,000 Iraqi and Saudi nationals to determine if any had ties to terrorist organizations. Nationals of some twenty-three other countries where al Qaeda is known to operate have been required to register with the authorities as well. The federal government is also actively tracking over half a million foreign students through its high-tech Student and Exchange Visitor Information System (SEVIS). And with the stroke of a pen, President George W. Bush decreed that nationals of Iraq and thirty-three other countries who seek political asylum in the United States can be detained throughout the time their petitions are being processed (which can take months, sometimes years). Meanwhile, the Bureau of Customs and Border Protection announced it would hire 2,000 new employees in a bid, as Homeland Security secretary Tom Ridge put it, to "seal our borders."

The scope of these measures—some of them unprecedented in American history—has had a dramatic impact on immigrant communities across the country. *Newsday* reported that hundreds of Pakistanis left their homes in the New York City region and fled to Canada to avoid having to register with the feds. One wonders what a Pakistani immigrant must think and feel when the government of his adopted land begins to take measures eerily reminiscent of his homeland's military dictatorship.

We say that America was changed forever on 9/11, that we "lost our innocence," a vague cliché. What certainly has changed is the way the world regards America, and the way we regard ourselves. If the War on

Terror, including the invasion and occupation of Iraq, has turned much of world public opinion against us, it also seems to have created a new set of borders within our borders. Since 9/11, we regard the strangers among us with something more than suspicion: it's more like outright paranoia. We Americans, yet again, are uncomfortable in our own motley skin.

Never in my entire life had I been so aware of my skin color and overall "ethnic" appearance as I was that morning in Maine. But clearly I was one of the lucky ones; there are dozens, perhaps hundreds—we have not been told by the authorities exactly how many—who remain in custody even as I write this, their constitutional rights suspended because, the Justice Department tells us, "we are at war."

The events of 9/11 shocked America because we had, in a sense, become insulated against the corporeal cruelty of the rest of the world. American exceptionalism had in many ways been bolstered by the fact that, since the Civil War, no blood had been spilled on our continental territory. Americans had come to claim an exemption from history, even as the rest of the globe remained steeped in its Joycean nightmare. Of course, some Americans never woke up from the nightmare—African Americans or anyone else who, within America's borders, lived as if in an occupied territory, unable to enjoy the rights and access supposedly guaranteed by the Constitution. American sociologist Frances Fukuyama may have declared the "end of history" a decade ago, but now in the early years of the twenty-first century, America has rejoined history with seemingly nineteenth century–style imperial fervor. The initial isolationist tendencies of the Bush administration have been swapped for an ambitious global campaign with both military and economic fronts—the War on Terror and the creation of free trade zones whose terms are decidedly favorable to the U.S. (and unfavorable to Third World nations). The architects of these grand designs seem to be proclaiming the sequel to our twentieth-century geopolitical and economic domination: the American Century, Part Two.

And yet, as always, there are contradictions in the American narrative, at home and abroad. President Bush speaks of bringing democracy to the world even as we make bedfellows of dictatorial regimes (Pakistan, Saudi Arabia) in the War on Terror. He speaks of waging war against those who "hate our freedom," and yet, under the "USA PATRIOT Act" and "Patriot Act II" passed by Congress in the wake of the terror attacks, many of our basic freedoms have been restricted. Our leaders rail against fundamentalisms abroad, and yet what is nativism if not an American brand of fundamentalism?

In addition to trade and national security, immigrants connect America to the world; indeed, they are the most poignant symbol of the impact of both our ideals and our policies abroad. Our moral standing in the eyes of the world may have taken a beating with our unilateralism in the wake of 9/11, but ask the immigrants—legal or illegal, professionals or unskilled laborers—why they come to our shores, and the answer is much the same as it was when Ellis Island was still the legendary port of entry for millions: in America, there is prosperity, in America, there is freedom.

In contrast to our immigration myths, Ellis Island wasn't exactly the most welcoming of places, and life in early twentieth-century tenements was no bed of roses. America has always been ambivalent about its newcomers, and it seems that these days the political pendulum swings more rapidly between the extremes of nativism and pluralism. The fallout from 9/11 is evident in the USA PATRIOT acts (of the tens of thousands of Arabs that registered with the federal government, some 13,000 are slated for deportation). At the same time, legislation that, if passed, would legalize millions of hitherto undocumented immigrants (most of them from Mexico) has been sponsored by high-profile politicos like

Senator John McCain, who also generally supports President Bush's foreign and homeland security policies.

Just as immigrants are ubiquitous in our everyday lives—we run into them at the car wash, they nanny our kids, they live in both our cities and in rural areas across the nation—so too are they present in every corner of our political life. To debate issues like citizenship, the minimum wage, healthcare, education, public housing, or whether English should be the official language of the U.S. inevitably invokes rhetoric that is pro- or anti-immigrant. A contradiction that began with the founding of the republic—the primordial political parting of the waters between who was and who wasn't considered a full American citizen—permeates our consciousness 228 years later.

::

The essays in this book are based on a PBS television documentary series that follows the lives of seven families in their journeys to America. I offer these words as context for why and how these people have moved, the circumstances under which they left one place and what they found upon arriving in another. As Americans, this narrative is familiar to us. We have long proclaimed ourselves a nation of immigrants, for indeed we are.

Mass migrations are nothing new in world history. The industrial revolution of the nineteenth century propelled millions from the provinces to the cities, from one country to another, across rivers, across oceans. What we are seeing today is akin to that great historical rupture. Many people fear this movement. Others celebrate it. Many others are conflicted about it.

My own identity is the product of this kind of movement. I am the son and grandson of immigrants from Latin America. My father's parents fled the chaos of the Mexican Revolution in the early twentieth century, eventually settling in Los Angeles. My mother made the journey from El Salvador to the United States in the late 1950s, escaping the political repression and instability of her native land. My parents met and married in Los Angeles, where I was born and raised.

From childhood and through my adult life, I have shuttled between my parents' Old Countries and my life in the "New World": California, land of perpetual immigrant hopes and dreams. My family's odyssey—from Old World tradition and poverty to the opportunity for social mobility and cultural transformation in America—took place over two generations. I am who I am today because of the interplay between history and momentous decisions based on individual will. I feel that my mixed parentage, my sense of connection to and independence from my family's Old World origins, is precisely what makes me an American.

This creed is what many Americans invoke as the basis of our national identity. And yet, we remain deeply conflicted about our immigrantness. The Statue of Liberty famously proclaims that America receives from the Old World ". . . your tired, your poor, your huddled masses yearning to breathe free, the wretched refuse of your teeming shore." But the immigrant rite of passage in America is just as famously arduous. We receive the first-generation stranger not with an open embrace but with mockery, with jokes and slurs and sweatshop wages, with inferior schools in the inner cities, and with harangues about "assimilation," with simpleton or savage representations on our movie and TV screens. Most of us who are Americans now were immigrants before, but a generation or two removed from the fact, we regard the "wretched refuse" with embarrassment.

The story of immigration is a nexus where myriad forces intersect, on both a societal and individual level, involving a dizzying set of causes and effects. "Push" factors such as poverty, civil war, famine, and political repression propel people across frontiers; they are "pulled" in by other factors, such as economies that benefit from the cheap labor that vulnerable migrants invariably offer, and are also inspired by the undeniably powerful cultural ideals of democratic nations. Colonial and postcolonial histories collide in the migrant story: the erstwhile colonial subject winds up on the streets of the "metropol," the former colonial seat of power. Like a Caliban running wild in the empire, he is resented because he is a troublesome reminder of colonial guilt and feared for the very same reason.

Much of my own life has been marked by these contradictions, even as a grade-school kid. I was in third grade in 1969, a time of cultural upheaval, but Black and Brown and Red and Yellow Power—the early discourse of what became, by the late 1980s, "multiculturalism"—had yet to trickle down into that most essential of public languages, the school curriculum. At Franklin Elementary, nestled at the base of the middle-class, mostly white hills of the Silver Lake district in Los Angeles, we received the typical liberal education of the era. We were taught the meaning of terms like "melting pot" and "assimilation," and indulged a primitive brand of multiculturalism by learning to sing "My Bonnie Lies Over the Ocean" and prancing about in a circle to the tune of the "Mexican Hat Dance" (the embarrassment I felt!). We learned that we were all the progeny of immigrants—except for the African slaves (but we were taught that great African Americans like Booker T. Washington salved the historical wound, and we had a friendly black janitor on our campus), and the poor Indians (whose disappearance was described less as bloody conquest than as unfortunate mishap for them, caught as deer in the headlights of Manifest Destiny). We understood that in America we were one under God, spoke one language and, despite our motley origins, we'd become one culture because the immigrants at Ellis Island turned in their Old World ways and emerged transformed. Difficult surnames were shorn, accents fell away, and Communist-leaning ideas pulled from one's head like rotten teeth. What did the immigrants get in the bargain? The future, of course: a one-way ticket into the middle class—provided you could pull yourself up by your own bootstraps.

One day a Mexican kid showed up at Franklin Elementary. (Surely his family's journey had been as momentous as my own.) He wore polyester to our American cotton, responded to our consonant-heavy English in the lyrical vowels of Spanish. Since I was the only bilingual kid in the school, I was assigned the role of interlocutor. I resented the task, which lasted the better part of the school year. He was an innocent deep-brown-skinned boy from the Mexican provinces, representing everything both sides of my family had hoped to banish from our future: the look, the smell, the very idea of poverty, and more than that, of the past, of that Old World past that, through American eyes, seemingly denies the future. My family had not undertaken this migration—a journey not just through physical but also cultural space and time—to be satisfied with an Old World existence inside the New. (Although, like all immigrant families, our cultural life was a constant negotiation of influences from both North and South.) We were in California (erstwhile Mexico, ironically) to stake a claim on the American exception.

In truth, I hated the little brown bastard (he was a shade darker than me) who invaded my turf at Franklin Elementary, because he reminded me and all the white kids and smattering of Asians at school of my ignominious origins. Seen through American eyes, Mexico was dusty, dirty, lazy; the vanquished Indian empire of the South. Me, I wanted to be a cowboy, just as my father had sided with the cowboys against the Indians in the Western flicks he was weaned on as a kid. I treated that boy terribly, denying in him what I denied in myself: history. Initially ecstatic at having a Spanish-speaker to commune with, the poor kid's gregarious manner quickly gave way to a morose silence. He was alone in America.

::

The immigrant has been our Other since before the founding of the republic. The core population of the colonies was not just Northern European, but over 90 percent British—overwhelmingly English and Scottish. Thus, the early United States exhibited both the rebelliousness and individualism of the early colonists—many of whom came to America precisely because they were outcasts back home—but also the colonial culture of the British empire, including its attitudes toward race, and these immediately found a target with the actual majority population of the region: Native Americans and African slaves. The early United States authored such enlightened documents as the Declaration of Independence and the Constitution, but was also, seemingly unaware of any contradiction, capable of propagating the institution of slavery and expressing virulent xenophobia.

American immigration history can be viewed in four epochs: the colonial period, the mid–nineteenth century, the turn of the twentieth, and post-1965. Each brought distinct national groups—and races and ethnicities—to the United States. The mid–nineteenth century saw mainly an influx from northern Europe; the early twentieth-century mainly from Southern and Eastern Europe; post-1965 mostly from Latin America and Asia.

Each epoch has seen its share of identity vetting. The earliest American settlers had only one real "other"—the Native Americans. Historians have noted a brief period of grace in the relation between Indians and whites in the earliest days of the colonies. For the white settlers, the gesture was more pragamatic than humanist. Since Columbus's time, Indians had been regarded as primitive and heathen, but for the first century of settlement, they were also crucial to the whites' designs on the continent—only through the Indians could the newcomers learn the lay of the land. As the settlers' thirst for more territory increased, so did their antagonism toward the Indian—and racial justifications for their extermination. The "noble" red man was rendered savage, an enemy to be vanquished, and the Indian Wars settled the deed.

But merely owning the land could not fulfill Americans' ambitions. The early nation had no export market to speak of, and an insufficient labor supply to create one. Thus began the importation of African slaves—for which whites had to invoke racial justifications yet again. Long before the first massive infusions of immigrants from Europe, the American psyche—the Anglo-American psyche, that is—already held firmly colonialist views of race, views that would affect the way the nation received Irish Catholics, Eastern European Jews, and Asians in the nineteenth century, and the cornucopia of non-Anglo groups throughout the twentieth.

These attitudes were not propagated by marginal or crackpot political figures. These were the attitudes of the founding fathers.

Take, for example, Alexander Hamilton, writing in 1802:

To admit foreigners indiscriminately to the rights of citizens the moment they put foot in our country . . . would be nothing less than to admit the Grecian horse into the citadel of our liberty and sovereignty.

Or even kindly Ben Franklin, back in 1751:

Why should the Palatine boors be suffered to swarm into our settlements, and, by herding together, establish their language and manners, to the exclusion of ours? Why should Pennsylvania, founded by the English, become a colony of aliens, who will shortly be so numerous as to Germanize us, instead of our Anglifying them?

Over two hundred fifty years later, anti-immigrant rhetoric is virtually unchanged. Here is British émigré (and naturalized American citizen) commentator Peter Brimelow, author of 1996's *Alien Nation:*

> It is immigration policy that has imported foreign ethnic conflicts, created impenetrable ethnic enclaves and mafias . . . overwhelmed the law enforcement agencies and—we will almost certainly learn—reduced the citizenship oath to a sick joke.

Shortly after the American Revolutionary War, the rhetoric was canonized as public policy with the Naturalization Act of 1790, which established a kind of American-style caste system: only immigrants of European descent could become full-fledged citizens. It would take nearly a century for the 14th amendment and the Naturalization Act of 1870 to afford citizenship to anyone born on American soil regardless of race; it would be almost 200 years later that the McCarran-Walter Act finally removed all racial barriers to immigration and citizenship.

Even the early years of the twentieth century, so often held up today as a nostalgic and heroic time of melting-pot triumphs, look different when viewed from the immigrant point of view. In Henry Roth's classic novel of immigrant travails, *Call It Sleep*, the Schearls, a family of Jewish émigrés, catch their first glimpse of Ellis Island:

> . . . before them, rising on her high pedestal from the scaling swarmy brilliance of sunlit water to the west, Liberty. The spinning disk of the late afternoon sun slanted behind her, and to those on board who gazed, her features were charred with shadow, her depths exhausted, her masses ironed to one single plane. Against the luminous sky the rays of her halo were spikes of darkness roweling in the air; shadow flattened the torch she

bore to a black cross against flawless light—the blackened hilt of a broken sword. Liberty.

This is not the Liberty of our mythology, but the frightful premonition of what life in the tenements of New York City would be like for the Schearls in 1907, the peak year of the first great migration of the twentieth century. Roth's novel was first published in 1934 and rescued from literary neglect in the early 1960s (when it became a huge bestseller), coincidentally around the time when the melting-pot ideal came into vogue. The Schearl family's tale is told through the eyes of young David, son of a doting mother and cruel father. There is no love or comfort in David's world except in his mother's protective arms. The streets of New York are cold, baffling, a labyrinth where danger lurks on every corner: street toughs, corrupt police, the chaos of the immigrant marketplace choked with pushcarts and exhausted laborers. So great is David's terror of the present that it is impossible for him to imagine a future, and he is too young to have enough of an Old World past to anchor him.

This narrative runs completely contrary to our notion of immigrant consciousness, precisely because it is told from the immigrant point of view. Most immigrant fables in America are told from the "native" perspective: Their purpose is to justify not just the American dream, but the historical toll it exacts on first-generation immigrants, on slaves, "people of color," women, anyone upon whose back the dream is built.

::

In his classic study *The Ethnic Myth,* urbanist Stephen Steinberg speaks of the "ignominious origins of [American] ethnic pluralism . . . in conquest, slavery, and exploitation of foreign labor." In contrast to our triumphalist mythology, Steinberg notes that migration begins with tragedy in the country of origin—in modern times, often a tragedy in which the United States is complicit (such as, say, the Central American civil wars in the 1980s) and continues tragically on streets paved not with gold but with a New World order of repression and fear, wherein immigrant desire is cornered by the forces of capital and the attendant institutions of the state (in the form of immigration authorities, local police, and welfare bureaucracies, to name a few).

If our national mythology invokes the immigrant as our historical and cultural Rosetta stone, why then is there such conflict surrounding the politics and culture of immigration? Why was the U.S.-Mexico frontier virtually open until 1924 (the year that the Border Patrol was first established), only to have hundreds of thousands of Mexican nationals deported barely a decade later in the Repatriation Program of the Depression years? Why did we allow the massive importation of Chinese labor to help build the railroads that opened the Western frontier, and then pass the Chinese Exclusion Act of 1882? Why did we grant "amnesty" to millions of "illegal" workers in 1986 even as we stepped up interdiction measures on the U.S.-Mexico border and sought to fine American employers if they hired undocumented labor? How is it that California, the multicultural state par excellence, came to pass the viciously anti-immigrant Proposition 187 in 1994?

The ambivalence cuts across virtually all lines of race, class, and even national origin. Take the experience of an unemployed African-American worker in the inner city: How can he avoid wondering if there is a connection between his plight and the arrival of cheap labor from the Third World? And among the immigrants themselves there is the classic divide between first and second generations and even between the recently-arrived and those who've been here longer: the fresh-off-the-boat immigrant is scorned by his brethren who arrived only a few years before him.

There is a connection between racism and xenophobia in America. Although historically African Americans have borne the brunt of discrimination, subsequent waves of immigrants have endured their share as well. Some still do, especially the "nonwhite" immigrants from Asia, Latin America, and Africa that are the core of the second great twentieth-century migration, which began with a liberalization of visa quotas in 1965. But depending on the particular time and place, even "white" immigrants can be "raced" and turned into a dark Other, such as Southern and Eastern Europeans in the early twentieth century and Eastern Europeans today (what with the Russians' reputation for gangsterism, a representation rapidly gaining currency in TV and film).

There is also a connection between racism, xenophobia, and social class in America. Although we call ourselves a "land of immigrants" and a "classless society"—the pillars of American exceptionalism—it is clear enough that economic disparity closely follows the lines of race, ethnicity, and national origin. Some groups, such as the Irish, Italians, and Eastern European Jews, endured intense discrimination as newcomers to this country but ultimately came to occupy middle-class economic status—and, equally important, a place in the cultural mainstream. Such experiences justify the ideal of the American dream: With enough hard work and sacrifice, the future is yours.

But what then, of the descendants of African slaves that remain socially immobile in the inner cities, or the Mexican-American families who have occupied the barrios in the Southwest for generations, or the Puerto Ricans in the ghettoes on the East Coast? Notwithstanding the image of Asians as the "model minority," there are pockets of deep poverty, especially among Southeast Asians, across America. All of this can be explained quite easily through a Social Darwinist perspective: "They" just don't have what it takes to make it.

Such pronouncements, however, ignore the economic and social factors at work both in the immigrants' countries of origin and here in the United States. Indeed, in the global era, the demarcation of economic status, unlike the restrictions on the flow of business capital and information, appears to be hardening rather than loosening. There have been decades of disinvestment in the kinds of public infrastructure that once offered the hope of creating a more level playing field for all in pursuit of their American dreams. The "social contract" that once offered a modicum of balance in the relationship between the interests of the state, capital, and labor has all but been abandoned, and in the "neoliberal" era, labor has clearly suffered most. For many immigrants, this state of affairs translates into something more than a "glass ceiling"; it is more like a brick wall standing in the way of social mobility. There is a fundamental paradox in all of this: Immigrants are both an expendable and irreplaceable class. Without their cheap labor, the expansion of Western economies would be impossible, but we are nonplussed as to what to do about the conditions they live in or work under, whether in Filipino assembly plants or in the neosweatshops of Los Angeles.

America's immigrant narrative continues to allow for success stories as well, although some of these are mediated by circumstances unforeseen by either immigrants or "natives." The army of foreign hi-tech workers in California's Silicon Valley, for example, would appear to have fulfilled all the requisites for being welcomed into the American family: extremely hard-working employees who know the American creed by heart. But many Americans, understandably, wonder why there aren't more qualified workers in the domestic labor pool. Ironically, even "model" immigrants like South Asian tech workers are resented precisely for their success.

And then there are the Horatio Alger rags-to-riches epics, such as superstar athletes who grew up in the most humiliating poverty and went on to become instant millionaires in American professional sports. Their stories are statistically very rare, of course, but nevertheless, we point to them as proof of all that is right about America. Out of all the immigrant images in our media today, theirs are easily the most celebrated. No one, after all, clamors for Sammy Sosa or Pedro Martínez to "go back where they came from." They stand on the American field of dreams, hands over their hearts, singing the "Star-Spangled Banner" and "Take Me Out to the Ballgame" right along with the rest of us. They might be black, they might be Dominican and speak with thickly accented English, but they are truly American heroes. And like all Horatio Alger tales, these narratives bolster the individualistic ideal that anyone can make it in America if they have what it takes.

::

The title of this book and the documentary series upon which it reflects proclaims that something is fundamentally different about our most recent wave of immigration. Experts point to 1965 as a watershed—the Immigration Act of that year altered nearly a century's worth of policy that had favored European nations with greater visa quota numbers, henceforth allowing vastly increased entries from the "Third World." But the authors of the 1965 legislation didn't foresee the American defeat in Vietnam (or the hundreds of thousands of "boat people" who would arrive on our shores). Or the Mariel boatlift from Cuba in 1980, or the Central American wars and their million-plus refugees, or the steady stream of Eastern European immigrants in the wake of the breakup of the Soviet Union, or the two most recent Mexican economic crises (1982 and 1994).

The racial and ethnic identity of the United States is—once again—being remade. The 2000 Census counts some 28 million first-generation immigrants among us. This is the highest number in history—often pointed out by anti-immigrant lobbyists—but it is not the highest percentage of the foreign-born in relation to the overall population. In 1907, that ratio was 14 percent; today, it is 10 percent.

Yet there is the pervasive notion that something is occurring that has never occurred before, or that more is at stake than ever before. And there is a crucial distinction to be made between the current wave and the ones that preceded it. As late as the 1950s, two-thirds of immigration to the U.S. originated in Europe. By the 1980s, more than 80 percent came from Latin America and Asia. As at every other historical juncture, when we receive a new batch of strangers, there is a reaction, a kind of political gasp that says: *We no longer recognize ourselves.* This is the mythical "middle American" speaking, of course, and he or she may be a white soccer mom in the suburbs or an African-American elder in the inner city, a young skinhead in Gary, Indiana, or even, on occasion, my father, the Mexican American, who, along with my mother, the Salvadoran American, briefly entertained restrictionist immigration notions in the early 1990s.

In response to this transformation, we've overhauled our immigration and border-enforcement policies several times in the past fifteen years. The landmark Immigration Reform and Control Act of 1986 (IRCA) is typical of our schizoid approach. Today, IRCA is remembered largely for the "amnesty" it granted some 2.7 million hitherto "illegal" or "undocumented" foreign nationals. The law, signed by President Reagan, offered permanent "legal" status and the possibility of full citizenship after a period of seven years to undocumented persons who could prove that they had lived and worked in the U.S. since 1982. In political terms, the amnesty provision of IRCA played to the compassionate image of Liberty and her open arms. But the anti-immigrant lobby in Washington also succeeded in making of IRCA a vehicle for "tightening the border." The "control" side of the law created the mechanism of "employer sanctions." Since 1988, everyone who applies for a job in the U.S., either in the public or private sector, must present "original documentation," such as a passport or birth certificate, that proves legal residency. Employers shown to consistently neglect the letter of this statute face fines and even jail time. (Convictions under the statute are rare, however; most "enforcement" of immigration law does not target American citizens who break the law by offering jobs to "illegals," but rather the immigrants themselves.)

After several years of economic decline, the 1990s ushered in, from the immigrant point of view, unmitigated negativity in the realm of public policy. Those were hopeless years for the California middle class, of which my family was a card-carrying member. Deindustrialization had devastated the Golden State's economic horizons, and many still recalled the fires of the Rodney King riots of 1992. To top it all off, the Northridge earthquake of 1994 and a series of spectacular wildfires on coastal hills and inland mountains seemed to augur apocalypse for California paradise. My mother and father eyed the real estate market tremulously as their California dream dangled over an abyss.

And one night my mother, a Kennedy liberal, said: "We just can't take care of all the world's poor." Meaning that it was time to batten down the hatches and keep the immigrants at bay.

Then-governor Pete Wilson invoked the age-old nativist platform and staked his political future on pointing the finger at the recently arrived immigrants (the vast majority from Mexico). In a 1994 TV campaign for the governor's reelection campaign, a dark voice intoned, "They keep coming," over grainy images of "illegals" stampeding across the U.S.-Mexico border. The rhetorical equation was simple: Too many immigrants equals a bad economy.

The economic arguments were merely cloaking more sinister racial ones. I was an immigration beat reporter in Los Angeles during that time, and I recall countless "man on the street" encounters with older (mostly white) Angelenos spewing forth complaints of how L.A. "looked like T.J.," that is, Tijuana, Mexico: the Third World-ization of the City of Angels.

Too many of *them*. Which is the flip side of not enough of *us*.

In the cacophony of debate toward the end of the 1994 election season, nativist crackpots with much worse to say aired their views not just on local talk radio but on the local news. I received "fan mail" for my political commentaries from people saying that Mexicans like me would take over California because we "breed like rabbits," and voicemail messages telling me to "go back to Mexico." (I, who was born in America.) I was aware that I was witnessing a replay of the age-old battle over the issue of immigration, over who is and isn't an American.

As hate mongers filled the airwaves, my parents, horrified, returned to their liberal roots, ultimately voting against Pete Wilson and the immigrant-bashing Proposition 187 (also known as "Save Our State," for the catchy acronym of "S.O.S.") he sponsored. Unfortunately for the immigrants, not nearly enough liberals did. Proposition 187 passed by a three-to-one margin. (Persons of Hispanic descent voted four-to-one against the measure, but their representation in the electorate has yet to match their growing numbers in the population; Anglo California voted four-to-one in favor.) While court injunctions held up enactment of the law (ultimately, most of it was deemed unconstitutional by both the California State and U.S. supreme courts), that didn't keep vigilantes from trying to enforce the codes on their own. Across California, hospital attendants and school officials began demanding "proof of citizenship" of anyone who "looked Mexican," from grandmothers with the flu to tots in kindergarten.

Responding to the clamor in California, the Clinton administration's Immigration and Naturalization Service (INS) implemented a new border strategy, which began with the construction of a nearly impenetrable steel wall on the line between Tijuana and San Diego. In one way, the wall serves a largely symbolic function, since it runs only eleven miles from the beach inland and beyond that point, for most of the next 2,000 miles, there are no such fortifications. But Operation Gatekeeper, as the strategy was called, had an impact on the migratory flow that was much more than symbolic. Like water seeking the path of least resistance, smugglers and their human cargo merely went around the wall, with deadly results. Eastern San Diego County along the border, where most illegal crossings in California have occurred in the wake of Gatekeeper, is highly rugged and isolated terrain, with brutally hot summers and frigid winters. Hundreds of migrants have died in their attempt to cross into the United States ever since the wall went up. Claiming "success" with Gatekeeper, the INS replicated the wall at several other points along the border in Arizona and Texas. The results have been deadly there as well. In the scorching summer of 2003, a record number of migrants perished in the area known as "el Camino del Diablo" (the Devil's Road) southeast of Tucson. Overall, an astonishing number of migrants— more than 3,000, or more than the number of civilians killed on 9/11— have died on the line in the last decade. The estimate, experts say, is a conservative one. There are many more bodies in remote regions of the desert, or on the bottom of the Rio Grande, that have yet to be found.

The anti-immigrant campaign continued with the Immigration Control and Financial Responsibility Act of 1996, which sought to deadbolt existing loopholes that allowed undocumented persons to remain in the country, and broadened the definition of who could be deported. Other contemporaneous pieces of legislation even targeted *legal* immigrants by capping the amount of public benefits they could receive.

By the end of the decade—as the economic boom became apparent and the political pendulum swung, ever so slightly, leftward—some of the public benefits were restored, and immigrant advocates on the Hill even passed a kind of closet "amnesty" with the so-called "245-i" rule, which allowed some 700,000 hitherto undocumented residents the opportunity to legalize their status—provided they had a "qualifying family member" (that is, an American citizen) to sponsor them. The loophole was obvious to all in the immigrant neighborhoods: Hundreds of thousands of people lined up across the country for marriages of convenience with American citizens. Such a shift in public policy—however murky and indirect—would have been impossible only a couple of years earlier, but despite heavy media coverage, no one complained much. The anti-immigrant lobby's message was lost in the "good times" feel of America's historic boom.

Then came 9/11 and recession. Predictably, immigrant-related legislation reached the White House in the wake of the terrorist attacks as the Enhanced Border Security and Visa Entry Reform Act of 2002. The law provides for more Border Patrol agents and demands that schools report foreign students attending classes. Furthermore, it stipulates that all foreign nationals in the U.S. will ultimately be required to carry identification documents that use biometric technology (such as retinal scanning). This piece of legislation clobbered the Restoration of Fairness in Immigration Act of 2002, a liberal proposal that would have, among other things, aided permanent residents trying to reunite families separated by "legal" and "illegal" status.

In the wake of 9/11, America continues to evidence its ambivalence over its immigrant history. Immediately following the attacks, the political leadership called for tolerance of ethnic and religious otherness, even as the FBI hunted down thousands of men of Arab descent. There has been, once again, a clamor for a national ID card, for stringent screening of those to whom we award the status of permanent resident, or tourist, student, and work visas, to "close the borders."

The real-world impact of our border policy remains deadly. In May of 2003, dozens of undocumented immigrants—ranging from pre-teens to elders—were crammed into a tractor-trailer after crossing the border in South Texas. Their smuggler, himself an immigrant (albeit a legal one, from Jamaica), apparently forgot to turn on the ventilation system on the long, hot ride to Houston. Nineteen migrants died as a result. The story made national headlines for its particularly high toll. But statistically speaking, at least one migrant dies on the border each and every day, his or her only epitaph a brief, sometimes nameless mention in a border newspaper.

Yet each of these deaths merits our attention. Never has there been such a toll on the U.S.-Mexico border. And hundreds, if not thousands, of prospective migrants have perished in Caribbean waters in recent years (on rickety rafts embarking from Haiti and Cuba). The idea of a journey to the New World has not been this harrowing—not, perhaps, since the Middle Passage.

Thus, for the immigrants, the symbols of America have been inscribed with new meanings over the centuries. Gleaming streets turned into shooting galleries (of bullets and drugs). The Statue of Liberty inspiring fear instead of hope. The Rio Grande no longer a River Jordan but a Styx.

And yet immigrants continue to arrive on our shores, no matter the risks, no matter the rhetoric from Washington or even the punitive legislation that makes life harder for the newcomers. After all, the essential "push" and "pull" factors remain in place. America is still a land of plenty in comparison to the rest of the world, because the rest of the world remains a dangerous place, a place where even to hope for something better often invites tragedy.

The issue of the immigrant, of who and what is an American, has never been resolved: It is an ongoing process, the molding of our identity. A new round of debate is upon us again. We will either shrink back from the challenge presented by the ideals of American democracy, or we will grow into our new immigrant selves.

In the following pages, we will meet men and women and children who are new to America, and who are agents of change in a New America. They hail from five different countries: Nigeria, the Dominican Republic, Mexico, India, and Israeli-occupied Palestine. As diverse as their origins are the circumstances of their journeys and the lives they have started here. For me, it is an opportunity to go beyond my own personal borders, to look for myself in the mirror of the faces that resemble mine the least.

1 :: **Palestine to Chicago** ::

Naima Saddeh and Hatem Abudayyeh

::

IT IS FOUR IN THE MORNING ON THE DAY OF HER DEPARTURE TO AMERICA, AND Naima Saadeh's cries—heaving sobs—echo through her family's modest home in the Palestinian West Bank village of El Jib. Her mother, sisters, and fiancé do their best to comfort her. Presently, she buries her head in her brother Jihad's chest. Naima is inconsolable, even though this is not actually a final good-bye to her family. Her sister will accompany her to the airport in Tel Aviv, and her mother and fiancé will board the flight to Chicago with her. But in the last several hours, there have been a series of wrenching farewells with friends and family. There's also been a stressful whirlwind of bureaucratic maneuvers to ensure Naima's visa is in order. If that wasn't enough, her university degree in Arabic Literature was imperiled when she failed a final exam on the Koran even as her fiancé arrived in El Jib to whisk her away to America. Finally, her pent-up emotions let loose.

In the weeks and months leading up to this day Naima has clung tenaciously to a vision of the future—a future she knows that she can only gain somewhere beyond her Palestinian village, beyond the Israeli occupied West Bank, far from the Middle East and its ceaseless conflict. She is tired of the authorities constantly asking her for her identity card, of petitioning those very authorities for permits to travel anywhere beyond the confines of El Jib. She has had her fill of prisoners and martyrs to the cause of Palestinian liberation, of Israeli elections that bring nothing good no matter which party wins, of checkpoints, of the intifada. So she spent years at university to stake a claim on a future as an educated woman. And she accepted a marriage proposal from an American-born Palestinian, Hatem Abudayyeh, an engagement that promises her love, companionship, and a one-way ticket to America.

But now, on the verge of departing, she realizes that the village life that she so often bemoans as hopelessly trapped by conservative tradition, is the only life she has ever known. She is a daughter of El Jib after all, and Chicago—her fiancé notwithstanding—is still an abstract notion. She has seen images of the great city, of course, and she imagined the cold wind from the Lake Michigan rushing down the avenues, but she cannot smell it like she smells the dusty breeze of the West Bank with its scent of olive groves, cannot touch it like she can touch the pages of the great works of Arabic literature she has studied, cannot hear it like the muezzin's call for morning prayers that crackles from the megaphones atop the minarets of the mosques or the ululating "cries of joy" of elder women when they receive good tidings that assure them that God does indeed remember His faithful in the humble village of El Jib.

Chicago is in the realm of the imaginary; only El Jib is real for Naima. Her body lives in the village and the village lives in her body. How, then, does she survive such a devastating journey away from home, as if she was cutting off one of her own limbs? The car will take her to the airport, the plane will carry her tens of thousands of feet into the sky and thousands of miles across the ocean—these are the simple things—and her body will arrive in that other world seemingly intact. But she will know that she has left something essential behind. Not just her family or her old house or the sights and smells of the village. It is something that is greater than the sum of these parts: history itself. Now she will be divorced from history, from her self. In America she will walk into another chapter of history and all the symbols will be rearranged, beginning with language. And language, she knows, is not just a set of words and their definitions; it is a way of seeing the world. How will she be able to see in this New World she is heading to? And how will the people of that world see her, she who comes from the Old?

::

Distance is one of the great ironies of the global era. If it is measured by time and space, technology in the digital age clearly diminishes the impact of the former on human communication. Naima and Hatem conducted much of their courtship via cellular phone, for example. When the young couple hit a snag in the paperwork at the American consulate—they needed Hatem's father's W-2 forms—Global Priority Mail came in handy. A video of their wedding in Chicago will soon arrive in El Jib; a family video from El Jib will make its way to Chicago. But technology does not mend a heart broken by distance in the spatial—the physical, as in corporeal—sense. A voice on the phone, an image on the screen, an E-mail, even an old-fashioned "hard copy" love letter arriving from afar: these things ultimately remind us of separation, of the impossibility of breaching the interminable space between us and our loved ones.

And what, then, of the time we thought we'd saved with our virtual communications? It seems to leak back into our lives, leading us back to notions of things irrevocable; it is a huge world after all. For most of us, at any rate. There are, of course, people that can breach both time and space, with enough money and frequent-flyer miles. But most global migrants do not have that luxury. The separations among migrant families are not measured in days and weeks, but in months and years, sometimes many years; occasionally, eternity. And so often in the lives of those who must seek their futures far from home, time inexorably leads to a very particular kind of tragedy: One day, the phone will ring in the wee hours in Chicago with news that a loved one has died in Palestine. On that day, the asphalt of the avenues and the angles of the skyscrapers and the wind off the lake will never seem as cold, so utterly impersonal and inhuman.

When will you return to El Jib, Naima? Will you again live in the village, as you sometimes fantasize with Hatem, on his family's property in that adorable little house now occupied by the old woman whose own home was confiscated by the Israelis in '48? Perhaps that is the question that cuts the deepest: You do not, and you cannot, know. What you do know is that, in the end, all your mighty efforts at actualizing yourself in the world do not ensure you will get what you want or even what you need. The rest is up to history, to the machinations of world leaders, to uprisings and occupations and treaties, to the rising and falling tides of the global economy. Everything you have done up to now has led you to this point—to this moment of departure.

"But you are going to America!" your sister says, trying to soothe you. Yes, you are leaving for America. Yet perhaps your pain rises from the fear that you will never really arrive, anywhere, again.

And now, your family does what families do best. Someone recalls a funny story about you, an incident that has nothing to do with the momentous occasion at hand, and, as such, it's the perfect remedy for the situation. Remember Ibrahim, Naima? Remember how he got sick with the runs and you tried to help him by giving him some tea? But you made a mistake, and you gave him *Bubanej*! You gave him a laxative! (The joke turns on Naima's bucking of tradition: Naima, no good at cooking, so awkward at a woman's work, her head in the clouds with poetry and big ideas!)

Everyone breaks out in laughter. And so do you, Naima, through your tears.

::

Hatem Abudayyeh speeds along the road toward East Jerusalem with the self-assurance of a native. But he is far from one. He was born and raised in Chicago, to parents who had emigrated from El Jib (his father left just before the 1967 Six-Day War; his mother left in its wake). His English is flawless, as befitting a second-generation kid educated in public schools. His haircut is fashionably short; he looks comfortable in his American casual wear. He plays a fair pick-up game at the gym with old high-school buddies, and enjoys a few beers at the local watering holes. The terms of who and what is an American these days might be a bit blurry, but in most respects, Hatem appears to be a young American through and through.

How is it that El Jib called to Hatem so strongly that he met and fell in love with Naima Saadeh? El Jib is not Hatem's hometown, after all; it is his parents' village. Arabic is not his first language; it is his parents' tongue. His is a Muslim family, but Hatem is more secular than devout (he likes pork!). And yet, Hatem dreams of living in Palestine one day. Is this a "roots" fantasy he will actually fulfill or that will remain a fantasy? Maybe he has internalized the longing he senses in his parents, who, like so many first-generation immigrants who swear they will return home, wind up living out their lives on American soil.

In the context of the Israeli occupation of Palestinian lands, these questions are all the more poignant. It is one thing to leave one's home-land behind because of a hurricane, famine, or even a civil war. Coun-tries eventually rebuild after a natural disaster; a country in the midst of a civil war is still a country—one side or the other wins, and life goes on for better or for worse. But Palestine is a country only in the haunted imagination of Palestinians living in the Occupied Territories or in exile.

As the late Edward Said, the preeminent scholar of the Palestinian diaspora, wrote:

[Does Palestine] exist? What proof do we have? The further we get from the Palestine of our past, the more precarious our status, the more disrupted our being, the more intermittent our presence. When did we become a people? When did we stop being one? Or are we in the process of becoming one?

Hatem was twenty-eight years old when he traveled to El Jib and met Naima, four years his junior. While his parents had always been actively involved in the Palestinian cause in America—they were even founders of one of the first Arab-American community centers in Chicago—Hatem also grew up comfortably middle-class. Although he studied English at UCLA, at the time he met Naima he was working as a waiter in a Chicago restaurant. He seemed to be drifting through his twenties.

The trip to El Jib was a watershed in Hatem's life. Within three weeks of arriving, he'd proposed to Naima and they were engaged. It was as if the lighthearted American boy, who said he'd "never had a stressful day," suddenly felt the weight of his life and his people's destiny. It wasn't only love that he found in the Old World village, it was history—or at least a part of the same history that Naima, an independent-minded woman in a harshly patriarchal society, was seeking to escape. And therein, it seems, lies the source of at least part of the attraction between Hatem and Naima: They sought opposite traits in one another. She desired the lightness of a New World freedom from history, and Hatem found in El Jib and with Naima the Old World gravitas that was missing in his life. There is something innately human about seeking in your intimate partner that which you lack in yourself. But when history provides such a dramatic backdrop for romance, the symbols can clash and create a tension that can either bind the couple or threaten to tear them apart.

Today's trip was supposed to be the simple fulfillment of a family obligation: Hatem's parents back home asked him the favor of calling upon an elderly woman who lives in a house they own in a Jerusalem suburb, to collect the rent. But for Hatem, the visit becomes an intimate encounter with the very history that sent his parents into exile and set the stage for Hatem's own birth in the States.

When Hatem and Naima first arrive, the woman leaves them alone while she slices some watermelon for her guests in the kitchen. Hatem rises from the sofa in the sitting room and quietly peeks into the adjacent rooms. He whispers to Naima that it's a cute little house, and they half-joke about living there one day. "Is it big enough?" Hatem says, smiling. The matron walks back in and sits before them. The small living room is utterly Old World: the sofa and coffee table seem to have been sitting there since before the war of 1948. The woman reminisces about Hatem's grandparents; it was his grandfather who built the house. But for the war, she would still be living in her own home, which was confiscated.

According to the United Nations Relief and Works Agency there are over three and a half million Palestinian refugees from the war of 1948, in which Jewish armies took control of most of the former Palestine. This number includes those Arabs who owned homes in the conquered territories as well as their descendants; today, the refugees live in the Occupied Territories of the West Bank and Gaza Strip, in other Arab states, especially Egypt, Syria, and Lebanon, and across the world: The Palestinian diaspora. The largest displacements took place after the declaration of Israeli statehood on May 15, 1948 (a date Palestinians refer to as "al Nakba," the catastrophe) and after the Six-Day-War in 1967, but Jewish migration into Palestine had begun decades earlier during the time of the British Mandate of 1917–1948. Palestinian insistence on the "right of return" for the refugees remains one of the key points of dispute in the Middle East peace process.

The old woman brings out a photo of what once was her home.

"There are hundreds of stories," Hatem tell us, "people who've never seen their homes, since they've been, how shall we say, 'resettled.'"

The woman tells of '48 in Arabic. Hatem translates:

"When they left as refugees, they didn't take anything from the house, no clothes, no money, they left everything, their furniture. . . ."

And then, suddenly, come her tears.

And then, surprisingly—or perhaps we shouldn't be surprised—come Hatem's as well. Both the woman and Hatem mirror each other, pinching their noses with thumb and forefinger and wiping their eyes repeatedly. For several moments, there is no sound but that of their very quiet crying. Now the woman rises from the sofa and walks out of the room, leaving Naima and Hatem alone again. Naima is the only one who hasn't shed a tear, although she is visibly moved. How many times has she heard this story? There would not be enough tears in her body, not enough in the Mediterranean Sea, to shed for each of the displaced of Palestine. What is she thinking about Hatem in this moment? That he is a very sensitive man? Or that he is still an innocent in the face of his own people's history? Or perhaps she thinks that his empathy cannot possibly run as deep as his tears would seem to indicate, this boy who grew up so far away, not in an occupied land, but in a place without checkpoints, in a *country*.

"Hatem loves Palestine," Naima says later. "And he would love to come live here. In the end I can see that both of us will come back and live here. But I'm a person who likes change. I want to change my life. I want to go and see the world."

And with that ambivalent declaration, Naima sums up the painfully confusing world she lives in and must find a way to navigate through: how to continue loving herself as she loves her village and family, even as she forsakes both by her journey to America.

::

Naima Saadeh has struggled her entire life against two equally powerful forces: the Occupation, and her culture's conservatism. To speak of tradition in a place like El Jib is to speak of thousands of years' worth of it. The village sits on land that was the site of the ancient city of Gibeon, referred to in the Old Testament as the place where, famously, the God of Israel made the sun stand still:

> When the Amorite kings of Canaan heard what the Gibeonites had done, they were alarmed. Said one, "Come up and help me attack Gibeon . . . because it has made peace with Joshua and the Israelites." So the five Amorite kings joined forces, moved their troops into position and assaulted the city. Besieged for help, Joshua ascended from Jericho and attacked the Amorite Kings, chasing them down to the valley of Ayalon and then praying to the Lord in front of all his people: "O sun, stand still over Gibeon, O moon, over the Valley of Aijalon." So the sun stood still, and the moon stopped, till the nation avenged itself on its enemies, as it is written in the Book of Jashar. The sun stopped in the middle of the sky and delayed going down about a full day. (Joshua 10: 12–13)

There is history that goes back further, of course. Ancient Palestine was another culture altogether, as matriarchal in its religious rites as the Israelites' were patriarchal. Among the pantheon of deities revered in the land of Canaan was Anat, "the goddess of heaven and earth," represented by the moon. Variously referred to as a virgin, a lover, a whore, and vengeful mistress, she was by most accounts venerated through much of the ancient Middle East. Palestinian poet Mahmoud Darwish invokes her as a symbol of a matriarchal Palestine lost to centuries of conquests by, among others, ancient Israelites, Greeks, Romans, Crusaders, Ottomans, British, and Zionists. Referring to Anat, he writes:

Wells dried up after you left us,
Streams and rivers ran dry when you died,
Tears evaporated from clay jars,
Air cracked like wooden embers from dryness,
And we broke down over your absence
Like fences rotting away.
Our desires have dried up
And our prayers turned to bone.
All is lifeless after your death,
For life died out like the conversations of
People on their way to Hell.
    —"The Phases of Anat"

Whether a goddess of fertility or a goddess of war, Anat is remarkable for her prolific role in the ancient narratives; she is a woman not just of passion but also of principles (such as her furious fealty to her brother Baal), and the will and strength to defend those principles—she leaves a bloody trail on the path of those who betray. It's not surprising that these qualities have made Anat something of a feminist icon in revisionist mythology.

And it is hard not to think of Anat when Naima displays her own feisty independence.

"I don't want to sound negative," she says. "But the people of El Jib are very conservative. They're bound by tradition and the need to conform. For example, I believe in God, but there are things that we need more than a new mosque—we already have two. We need a recreation

KARTEMQUIN FILMS

Naima and her mother, Um Mujahid, in El Jib

center for young men and women. But with the backward state of mind here, how could a young woman leave the house to use it?"

At university, Naima, unlike most of her colleagues, does not wear the traditional *hajib*, or veil (although she remains a practicing Muslim). She dresses smartly in pantsuits and vests, very much the modern woman—

or, at least, with as much modernity as she can muster in a small Palestinian village. It's quite a sight to see her walking along the stone-strewn paths, past flocks of sheep and the occasional camel in her professional-woman attire. Sometimes, she lets her full, raven-black hair down in public. And she is not afraid to speak her mind. In her literature classes, she is often the first to thrust her hand up to answer a question from the invariably male professors.

But there is another Naima, who remains her mother's daughter and daughter of her village, no matter how much she tries to squirm out of the role. At home one day before her departure, the women of the family are rolling grape leaves in the kitchen.

"I hate doing this," Naima says in the midst of a halfhearted attempt to complete a decent grape-leaf roll.

"But you still have to do it!" snaps her mother.

Naima's niece Ishan, quite sharp at the age of five, moves in for the kill.

"Isn't [Hatem] your fiancé? You have to cook for him, right?"

"That's right!" Mom cries, triumphantly.

Now Naima's sister Shafeeka, Ishan's mother, joins in the needling.

"Yeah, doesn't every woman cook for her husband?" she says. Ironically, today Shafeeka is dressed in a T-shirt and backwards baseball cap, quite the "b-girl."

"No," says Naima finally, but without much verve. There is no winning this battle, at any rate not here, at her family's home in the village.

The Saadehs are an intensely tight-knit family—not unlike most Old World families. The intimacy is physical as well as emotional. In lands where underdeveloped public institutions fail the people at every turn, where the public life itself is a source of persecution rather than of community, the family is the only support system you have. Americans can talk about "family values" all they want, but the typical American family's brand of intimacy—gathering, with luck, for year-end holidays, weddings, and funerals—seems utterly alien in the Old World context. I know for certain that I am an American when I visit relatives in El Salvador and feel claustrophobic after only a few days of round-the-clock family socializing.

Naima's father died in a car accident when she was two years old, leaving her mother, Um Mujahid, to raise five girls and two boys, a monumental task for any woman and more so for a widow in an occupied, poverty-stricken territory. Luckily, Um Mujahid secured a job as a laundress at the Dar Al-Tifl school for orphans in Jerusalem, founded by a woman of means named Hind Husseini in the wake of '48. The story goes that after the Deir Yassin Massacre, in which the Stern and Irgon Zionist brigades killed 250 civilians, Husseini came upon ten forlorn orphans on the street and was so moved that she vowed to make a home for them. For ten years, Naima's mother lived in the servants' quarters on the Dar Al-Tifl campus, working in the kitchen and doing laundry. Altogether, Um Mujahid worked at Dar Al-Tifl for 19 years.

"If she could give us her soul, she would give us her soul," Naima says of her mother. "And I wish that I could give her what she has given me—and more."

When the first intifada broke out in 1987, both of Naima's brothers took to the streets against the Israeli occupation forces; both were jailed and her oldest brother, Mujahid, died in prison under mysterious circumstances; he was just 21 years old. Jihad, the younger of the brothers, survived his own stint in prison. During his three years in confinement, he corresponded with the family by smuggling letters out of prison. These were written in tiny print on tissue paper. When other prisoners were released, the letters were tightly folded and wrapped in plastic like a capsule, which the departing prisoner would swallow.

"Don't pay the bail!" he wrote the family once. "We need the money more than the Jews do." In an interview, Jihad says that it wasn't so much the money that was the issue. For Jihad, paying the bail would be a symbol of "giving in to the Occupation."

At times, Jihad, still only 25 years old, is sanguine about the experience.

"Prison is like a flower that everyone in Palestine has to smell," he says.

Jihad also says that "99 percent" of young Palestinians want to leave their homeland. "And I would round it off to 100 percent." Still, most have little hope of travel even within the Occupied Territories, much less of emigrating. Naima is one of the lucky ones.

Today, Jihad makes a living replacing windows, a job that often takes him to an Israeli settlement just up the road from his village, a cruel irony—as if he were still serving his former jailers. And like most Palestinians who've never been to America—like most people in the "developing world" who've never been to America, for that matter— Jihad has visions of a shining city on a hill, a place where his sister will find happiness.

"There are no complications over there," he says. "No checkpoints. People are free."

Jihad, like the rest of the family, looks upon Naima's impending journey as a redemptive act for the entire clan. It's as if, with the failure of the Palestinian resistance—and by extension the failure of Jihad's role as a fighter in the resistance—Naima's success at university and chance at the American dream fill the void of the lost homeland.

On some level, of course, Naima is aware of her family's hopes and dreams being conflated with her own. Imagine Naima's burden: She was raised in a fatherless, impoverished household. She is an independent-minded woman in a patriarchal society, and the daughter of a country that is not named on any modern map. Little wonder, then, that as her final semester at university winds down and Hatem arrives in El Jib for the final bureaucratic push to get her papers in order for the trip to America, her stress becomes unbearable.

There is Naima's long wait in line at the American Consulate only to be told by the Consul herself that her paperwork is not in order. (Hatem makes an urgent call to Chicago: his father, officially Naima's "sponsor" in the U.S., must send his W-2 forms to prove his solvency.) Then there is a trip to an Israeli government compound in Ramallah to secure travel permits for her mother and sister so that they can accompany Hatem and Naima to the airport in Tel Aviv (her mother will travel with her to Chicago; her sister will go as far as Tel Aviv for "support"). After another exhausting wait in the midday sun, they are told that the office has run out of permits and that it'll take a few hours to print up more.

There is also the wedding to think about, of course. At home in her bedroom Naima and her sisters Ismahan, Shafeeka, and Khawla lounge on the bed and browse through a stack of American bridal magazines containing the latest fashions—mostly sleeveless, backless and low-cut, the kind of smoldering sensual look a Julia Roberts or Jennifer Lopez would wear to the altar, not an Old World daughter. There's a hilarious moment when Jihad comes in and is asked to pick out a dress for his sister. His clumsy choice—he picks a style fit for a conservative matron—causes a fit of laughter among the sisters. But there's a hint of trouble ahead, even on this joyous occasion: Jihad's choice would probably meet their mother's approval. The Jennifer Lopez look would not.

"If only Mom will accept it," one of the sisters says. "But the top is too low!"

(The New World—Naima—tussles with the Old—her mother—even in the Old World.)

And then the unthinkable happens. Naima, by all accounts a diligent student at Jerusalem University, fails a final exam on the Koran. She is told that she cannot graduate and receive her degree unless she passes a makeup. It is a crushing blow, especially for Naima's mother. Hardly a day goes by that Um Mujahid does not talk about how she's worked her fingers to the bone all these years so that her children could secure an education. ("The girls' education is the most important thing," she says. "I swore I'd keep working until Naima finished at the university.") Mom herself cannot read or write—when she must sign one of the myriad forms for her visa, Hatem, holding her hand, helps her scrawl a signature. The intifada took one of Naima's brother's lives and left the other scarred by prison. Her three sisters in Palestine live humbly, and while they've all gone on to college, they harbor few illusions about their future: History, in the form of the Occupation, the intifadas, keeps getting in the way. The eldest Saadeh sibling, Sanaa, was the first and only of the clan to emigrate to America before Naima, and she will soon finish a B.A. at Northeastern University. At the very least, Naima must live up to Sanaa's example. But now Naima's degree—the very symbol of her ambition—is suddenly in question.

Now that Hatem is in El Jib, the momentum toward Naima's departure is unstoppable, and her strong-willed personality begins to show cracks. In her final days in El Jib, she breaks into tears repeatedly, mostly when she's in the presence of Um Mujahid. Naima's face is often tightened with anxiety, lips pursed, nary a smile or laugh.

And then, liberation. Naima takes the makeup exam on the Koran. The professor corrects it in front of her (one can imagine the nail-biting). She passes: She is a college graduate. At home, the celebration immediately gets underway with Naima's mother uttering the "cries of joy," poetic verses of praise to God for bringing good tidings:

My heart was broken
But now it is healed . . . aaaeiiiiiiiiii!

The good news spreads, the family gathers at home. Naima collapses into her sister's arms with tears of relief and joy. Tea is served. Jihad arrives, kisses his mother on both cheeks and smiles wide: "Congratulations on your daughter's achievement!"

There is more ululating, so that the whole neighborhood, the entire village, might know the news. Even Naima's niece Ishan joins in on the act, dancing in the living room as Mom and Jihad tap out a beat on the tabla, and adds her own cry of joy about Naima's impending union with Hatem. In doing so, she reminds everyone that there is more to celebrate than just the college degree. A daughter is marrying. A daughter is making her way to America.

::

The celebration lasts well into the warm summer evening. As usual, the party splits along gender lines. The men hold court outside and talk about—what else?—politics and Palestine. Hatem listens intently as the men, mostly in their twenties and thirties, go back and forth.

"The U.S., that's what's best for me," says one. "Everything, they have everything there. I love being Palestinian, and I love Palestine, but what I want as a human being I can't achieve here. I want a good life, good education, and good work. And I want to find my dignity through work."

Replies another: "He's the first person I've met that's going to look for his dignity in the States." The comment prompts laughter from the group and a red-faced smile from the America enthusiast.

Hatem protests. "I will tell you, you will not find dignity there. It is the most racist country in the world."

This is not the Hatem we are used to hearing. His Palestine sojourn, clearly, is having an impact on his political awareness of both his homelands. He will return to America with this rekindled passion, and it will alter the course of his and Naima's life.

"I stand on the stairs of Damascus Gate and smell the air," says another man, wistfully. "The smell of Jerusalem makes me feel like staying in Jerusalem."

Now Jihad, who claims no little authority among the group as a veteran resistance fighter, speaks up. "You are free to feel what you want," he says, looking at Hatem. "As for myself, I served my country and now I want to leave."

Hatem protests, notwithstanding his lack of political credentials here as the American-born Arab: "But the problem for Palestinians is that others want to take our land, and if we run away they will take it!"

Jihad spits out bitterly: "Let them take it!" It's a slap to Hatem's romantic notions of the resistance.

Jihad again: "All the land inside the walls of Jerusalem has already been sold . . . and that means they will never give it back to us."

Another man offers: "We know that there are many problems here. It doesn't mean you should just pick up and leave."

But Jihad will have none of it. "I think I've completed my role here. And now I need to look for other opportunities."

"But you're running from the occupation," someone else chimes in.

"No," Jihad hisses, beads of sweat breaking out on his forehead. "I'm not running from the occupation. A country that has no sea, who needs it? We have no sea."

"What about Gaza?" someone says.

Jihad cuts him off: "You can't even go to Gaza, you're not allowed! They took the entire oceanfront."

"What about the people that died defending this country?" offers another. "Were they stupid?"

"Yes, they were stupid and idiots, I swear!" Jihad shouts, the anger finally cresting. "If they were using their heads, they wouldn't have done that."

"But you were in prison," the same man protests.

"I was clueless, too," Jihad replies, with no choice but to swallow his own venom. "I didn't know that this is what would become of my country."

Silence for a beat as everyone wrestles in their hearts with their deepest desires and the forces that hold them forever out of reach. "We're obviously a very depressed and angry people," says a young father, cradling his baby. "But as long as the people themselves don't change, we'll continue, living in conflict."

There are not many choices in an occupied land. Stay. Go. Accommodate. Resist. Go, stay, resist, accommodate.

Hatem remains quiet, watching the back-and-forth intently. On his face is a look that tells us that something is being revealed to him. Something that he's always known in the abstract, but now, here in his homeland, with these men trapped in the cruelest of histories, it is all too real.

"I don't want to fight anymore," says Jihad desperately, defeated. "I'm sick of it. I just want to get out of here."

::

It is afternoon on the day before Naima's departure. At home the suitcases are open. Along with the clothes are the inevitable gifts from the homeland for relatives in the distant land. The smell and taste of home for those far from home. In a series of Pepsi liter bottles and plastic bags, Naima's mom packs the delicacies: Yogurt, almonds, pickled cucumber, cracked wheat, chamomile. These things are readily available at Arabic and even American stores in Chicago, of course. But when a loved one brings them from home, the taste is all the sweeter.

I remember the occasions when my grandparents arrived in Los Angeles from El Salvador with dry, salty cheeses, thick Central American–style corn tortillas, buttery-sugary pastries. The unpacking of these gifts was always the first order of business as soon as we got home from the airport. The moment the suitcases were opened, the aroma not just of the foodstuffs but also of every article of clothing, magazine, and curio from home would permeate the room. It was a musty-sweet smell that recalled palm fronds, ceiba bark, moist black earth, the ground mists of morning, and the towering cumuli of the afternoon, women walking alongside the road balancing baskets of fresh tortillas on their heads. My memory of these things was twofold: I knew the Old Country because of our frequent visits, but I also imbibed my mother's remembrances, the homeland that lived in her even as she shaped her American future 3,000 miles from home.

My mother would brew some coffee (from the beans just unpacked from the suitcase), and the reunited family would sit around the dinner table, savoring every sip and bite of home.

::

Welcome to America, Naima! Welcome, with Customs agents and gleaming luggage carousels and cellophane balloons and flowers and extended family ululating, with Chicago's elevated trains and the wind off the lake! The Statue of Liberty is not at O'Hare to greet you, but she might as well be; you know the inscription by heart like the rest of the world does. You are among the Tired, the Hungry, the Huddled Masses Yearning to be Free now given refuge under the torch of liberty, under the golden arches of McDonald's, with reruns of *Friends* and debates

In Chicago

over which commercial was best at Super Bowl halftime. After all those years in the Occupied Territories, the future you yearned for has become present: and, of course, you weren't prepared for it. No one ever is, could ever possibly be.

Compared to most new arrivals, your passage is a relatively easy one. Your mother sat next to you on the jet and will remain with you for your first year in America (and your first year of marriage). Your sister Sanaa lives in Chicago, with two of your nephews. Your fiancé, Hatem, has remodeled the basement of his family's building into a private and comfortable apartment.

Yes, compared to most new arrivals, yours has been a safe, warm passage. No harrowing illegal journey across the Mexican border with unscrupulous smugglers, no raft ride across the treacherous Caribbean sea like the Haitians, Dominicans, or Cubans. Not even like my own mother, arriving absolutely alone in America from her native El Salvador in 1957.

But of course one's experience of migration is not measured by an objective standard. And your journey—which, really, has just begun by arriving in America—is and will be a painful and confusing one.

You, who studied English so diligently in your homeland, will find yourself stuttering the consonants and stumbling over vocabulary as you attempt to translate your mature, nuanced thoughts in Arabic into the bizarre idiom of colloquial American English. You, the feisty and confident woman who bucked tradition in El Jib, will suddenly find yourself feeling and acting tentative, awkward. The elation of your whirlwind romance with Hatem will wear off and real life—with all its little and sometimes large annoyances—will settle in.

The future is yours. You just don't know what it means anymore.

::

The wedding is in three weeks, and it is time for Naima Saadeh, soon to be Naima Abudayyeh, to shop for a wedding dress in Chicago. Her mother and her sister Sanaa accompany her to the bridal shop. It is here where the first of many battles between Old World and New takes place. The first dress Naima tries on is low in front. Mother ticks her displeasure. The next is high in front but low in back. Mother shakes her head again. Now a conservative dress that delights Mom and horrifies Naima. "God forgive me for my opinions, I won't say anymore," Um Mujahid says over and again, just before offering a new view on the depravity of one low cut or another. "Don't worry, she's going to wear something acceptable," Sanaa tries to reassure her. But it seems that there's no way to reassure her. Um Mujahid, at least on matters of feminine style, is a strict Muslim, and it's clear she fears the influence of secular, sexy America on her daughter. It is probably at times like these when Naima wishes she was on her own in America, free to find herself in the language and style of her new home.

But then there are times when Naima is very much her mother's daughter after all, especially in her relationship with Hatem. The passion of long-distance love has begun to give way to a quotidian relationship. Religion becomes a particularly sore point between them, between Naima the devout and Hatem the secular. Shopping at the supermarket, Hatem drools over a package of pork bratwurst, to Naima's disgust. "How can you have a taste for this ugly thing?" she complains. "No uglier than a cow," Hatem responds. In fact, Hatem seems to enjoy occasionally but consistently ribbing Naima about her faith rituals. At home, he will make jokes while Naima and her mother listen to audio tapes of Koranic readings. At times like these, Hatem seems every inch the American whose belief in the civic religion of democratic ideals is paramount.

In the days leading up to the wedding, while the women are busy mixing henna for the ceremony that welcomes the bride to the family of the groom, Hatem makes the point to anyone who will listen that he will buck tradition by refusing to don the *hatah*, the traditional Arab headdress for formal occasions. To Hatem's credit, it is a fairly principled stand, saying that it "represents the Gulf states, and I don't particularly like their politics."

But come the day of the wedding, Hatem appears, the white *hatah* crowning his formal suit and tie. Ironically, it is Naima who bends the rules of tradition at the wedding: she chose the low-cut gown after all, to the consternation of her mother. Yet the ceremony itself is a grand spectacle of tradition, with the women ululating and the men clapping while Naima dances solo, carrying two long burning candlesticks, her beautiful gown showing a hint of cleavage but with its long folds elegant enough to elicit admiring sighs from family and friends. For the occasion, Hatem and Naima put aside their symbolic, petty differences. It is a beautiful wedding, nary a forced smile from bride or groom or anyone else. It is a moment in which a wedding hall in Palestine is recreated in Chicago, Illinois, the will of a community—with Naima and Hatem at its heart—making of the imaginary a living, breathing, loving thing.

::

After a honeymoon on a Mexican beach, it is now time for Naima and Hatem to go about the details of their new lives, which they are starting from scratch. There is furniture to buy for their basement apartment, clothes for Naima's first frigid Chicago winter, and the small matter of both husband and wife finding jobs. Naima's first interview for a position at a battered women's shelter goes badly. Her English is halting, and she asks that one of the two interviewers, who speaks Arabic, translate for her. In the end, she is offered only a volunteer position. Her second job opportunity at the University of Chicago's Center for Middle Eastern Studies finds her being lectured by a professor to improve her language skills. "You are very courageous," he tells her, after making it clear that there would be no job offer. "There are many and limitless possibilities in this country, but it requires hard work."

Her first experiences in the job market leave Naima's confidence at an ebb. "In Palestine, I can do everything. Since I was a child, I do everything without any help, and suddenly I find myself, I can't do even a little bit. I want to start feeling like I'm making a contribution."

At work in Chicago

When she finally does land her first job, it is not because she's improved her English. She is hired as an Arabic language teacher for youth at a Muslim school.

Predictably, Hatem fares better in the job market. The job he secures owes much to his family's high standing in the Chicago Arabic community: He is hired as director of youth programs for the Arab American Action Network, the organization his own parents helped establish not long after leaving Palestine. The job is as meaningful to Hatem as his last job, waiting tables, was meaningless, and it is another step forward in his blossoming consciousness. Things seem to be falling perfectly into place: He professes utter joy at being married ("I don't know why I spent so much time avoiding it!") and in his job.

::

It's the more mundane moments that Hatem has a harder time with, and these usually have to do with Naima's process of acculturation. Like Hatem attempting to teach Naima how to drive. He sits in the passenger seat, white knuckling, barking out orders like a field commander.

"Stop . . . *stop!* You didn't stop!" he shouts when Naima passes the limit line at an intersection.

But Naima does not take his condescending impatience without jabbing back.

"I don't like it when you yell at me," she says, still stopped at the intersection. "I didn't do anything wrong."

But Hatem himself can't be wrong, and he persists: "If a kid runs into the street, you have to be able to stop, right?"

And Naima matches him: "Why don't you run in front of the car, and we'll see if I can stop."

It's a hilarious retort, but Hatem only curls his lip in the slightest of smiles.

For all his self-assurance, now and again Hatem shows that he's an awkward young newlywed as much as Naima. On one of their first outings to the Laundromat, he empties the better part of a box of detergent into a machine. The resulting explosion shuts down the washer, a sea of suds spills across the floor, and Hatem and Naima look every bit like Lucy and Ricky.

The Midwest winter passes slowly. Naima suffers the bitter wind off the lake, but has fun making snowballs to throw at Hatem, and the couple have a great night out at an outdoor skating rink, Naima dramatically spilling across the ice again and again, taking Hatem down with her in fits of laughter.

::

By springtime, Naima's made great strides in adapting to her new home. She speaks English ever more confidently, and, after more tutoring from Hatem, masters Chicago's transportation system. During the week, she takes a combination of trains and buses to her summer job tutoring students studying Arabic at the University of Chicago, and after work makes the trek to her evening classes in English.

Naima's mother, however, remains trapped in the Old World, a place it is clear that she will never leave, whether or not she physically remains in America. By and large she stays in the Abudayyehs' apartment all day long, providing day care for her sister's children. She makes not so much as a trip to the store alone.

"Old people stay home here," she says. "It's only good for people who work, time passes for them, but I just stay home and don't do much. Back home I used to walk around, visit people, go everywhere, but now I have to wait for my sister to come back to do anything."

Clearly, acculturation is a matter for the young. Um Mujahid reminds me of my own Mexican grandmother. Both she and my grandfather relied on my father for translation and navigating the New World's bureaucracies. They came to speak English only haltingly and with thick accents. They bought a handsome home in a Los Angeles middle-class neighborhood, but their neighbors never considered them Americans. I don't think that they considered themselves Americans, either. They were born Mexicans in Mexico and died Mexicans on American soil.

Naima and Hatem's experience of what was once called the "melting pot" points to the complexities of migration and the negotiation of cultural identity in the global era. The great irony of the times is that, although the onslaught of American pop culture is felt everywhere from London to Tokyo to Beirut, it's not as if the indigenous cultures have simply withered and disappeared; if anything, the sense of nationalism and regionalism is emboldened not just in the primordial homeland but in the second or third or fourth homes of the global exiles as they move and are moved by desire and the economy. In some ways, today's travelers are following in the footsteps of the migrants of yore, establishing their enclaves and using their indigenous culture as a shield against the alienating aspects of immigrant life in the new country. But I suspect that there's more to it than that. What Americans have never understood is that the rest of the world's attitude toward this country is neither utter anti-Americanism, nor its opposite, the utter adulation of all things American. Most people are ambivalent, and logically so: An Arab can groove to our pop music and still resent us for our militarism in the Gulf and decades of support for Israel.

With the collapse of the Eastern Bloc, the Third World watched America carefully. Would the world's only superpower live up to its ideals on the international sphere, now that the old Communist bogeyman was gone and with him the justification for the support of murderous regimes the world over? American's recent diplomatic and military history has not inspired too much trust in most corners of the world. We intervene not out of moral obligation but out of narrow self-interest; diplomatic and military commitments must rise to the level of "national interests" or "national security." Bosnia met the criteria; Rwanda didn't. We invaded Iraq a second time because we said Saddam Hussein posed an imminent threat to world order, but we still speak of other brutal regimes in the Middle East (Egypt, Saudi Arabia) as our "friends." One can only wonder what impact the neo-Reaganite big stick of the early twenty-first-century American empire will have on matters of global culture. Americans may very well continue to "orientalize" (to use Edward Said's term) exotic cultures, as befits our standing as a neo-colonial empire. The rest of the world's long-standing love affair with

American pop culture, however, is showing signs of wearing thin. There may be fewer and fewer global megastars of the Madonna and Britney variety. There may be fewer and fewer points of encounter between "us" and "them." And because of the recent, massive immigrant infusion from the Third World, these tensions may increasingly play themselves out in America itself. In the 90s, this prospect was referred to, often by neoconservatives, as "Balkanization." The tug of war over who is (and how one becomes) an American remains.

And so Naima and Hatem negotiate their identities like the characters on the global stage that they are. Hatem's job at the Arab American Action Network and the outbreak of the second intifada pushes him into a very public role as an advocate of the Palestinian cause in Chicago. He approaches the task with an almost religious fervor, but his American-ness shows through in his insistence on secularism. Naima, on the other hand, clings to her Muslim spiritual practice—it seems to be the peaceful center of her otherwise chaotic new life in America. During Ramadan, she observes the fasting rites. One morning during the holy days, Hatem gives her a ride to her job at the Muslim school. As Naima is about to get out of the car, he leans over to give her a kiss. But she pushes him away: Part of the fasting ritual is abstinence in the intimate sense. She covers her head with her *hijab* and exits the car, leaving Hatem shaking his head.

Even the issue that would seem to provide the couple with common ground—the cause of Palestinian liberation—is a source of tension. Hatem arrives at home one evening with a photograph that he'd like to put up somewhere in the apartment. It's a troubling image of two elder Palestinian women; no folkloric shot this one: It's a graphic rendering of pain and rebelliousness in the face of the Israeli occupation. Hatem walks into the entryway and asks Naima's opinion of placing it there, and she immediately protests.

For Hatem, it's a righteous statement: "So as soon as anyone walks in, they'll know what we're about."

For Naima, it's a tired representation of a struggle she's weary of. "We have enough sadness," she says.

"And we need more," Hatem replies. "We need it until it's over; we need to struggle until we win."

Now the argument heats up. "Two hundred years," Naima says with exasperation, recalling her brother Jihad's comments to Hatem a year ago in El Jib. "A million years, for what? For nothing."

There is a pro-Palestinian demonstration in Washington, D.C., soon, and Hatem is committed to making the trip. He invited Naima, who originally said yes. Now she tells him she doesn't want to go.

Hatem protests: "But you lived in the middle of it! How could you feel like you want to give it up? We have a responsibility to those people. . . ."

Naima cuts him off: "Maybe you know more than me."

This is obviously a bitter pill for Hatem: Part of his desire for Naima in the beginning had to do precisely with his nascent political awareness and his romanticization of *jihad* overseas. But Naima did not come to America to continue that struggle. She came here, like so many new Americans, to wage a struggle of a very different kind: to break free from the chains of history, to place the "I" before the "we." And Hatem, of course, who's grown up in the land of the "I," very much wants to feel part of the "we."

It is an old argument that has no quick resolution, of course; perhaps it is a tension that can never be resolved. To a great degree, it seems, this negotiation will determine whether Naima and Hatem's love can rise above history . . . or at least make peace with it.

The Narrative of Exile :: **Mahmoud Darwish**

I'm thinking of El Salvador as I read Mahmoud Darwish's poetry.

In most quarters, Darwish is referred to as the "poet of the Palestinian people" – an unenviable mantle to carry, especially for an artist as complex as
Darwish, who has wrestled with the ideals of "resistance" poetry and the contrary dictates of his magnificent lyric imagination.

According to biographical information in the excellent translated poetry collections *Psalms* (edited by Ben Bennani) and *The Adam of Two Edens* (edited by
Munir Akash and Daniel Moore), Darwish was born in Birwa, a small village in
Galilee. He was six years old when fighting broke out in 1948, and had his first
taste of exile that year when his family fled, literally under a hail of bullets, to
Lebanon. Nearly two years later, they returned to Palestine – without permission – to find their village destroyed. The Israeli authorities, in Orwellian fashion, designated Darwish and thousands of others like him "present-absent
aliens." When he was eight years old, he composed a poem about the
Palestinian situation that he read aloud in school, for which the Israeli military
governor promptly browbeat him. Throughout his adolescence and early adult-
hood, he was frequently harassed, placed under house arrest, and imprisoned
by the authorities for his literary and political activities – in Darwish's case,
there could be no distinction between the two. The "crime" he usually committed was traveling without a permit, which Palestinians must secure for journeys of any purpose beyond their villages. Darwish's requests for permits – for
such occasions as poetry festivals and Muslim feasts – were almost always
denied. But Darwish himself would not be denied, hence his "illegal" travels
and their juridical consequences.

Some years ago, in El Salvador, I knew a poet who had Darwish's spirit.

Through much of the 1980s, I shuttled between my hometown of Los
Angeles and my mother's hometown of San Salvador. Some of my earliest

memories are of harrowing Pan American flights through the turbulent tropical air above Guatemala and El Salvador. Other early memories are of devastating poverty: I'd see beggars, boys my age dressed in rags, barefoot and
gaunt, and ask my grandfather how there could be such a huge material difference between their and my lives. My grandfather was a kind and gracious
man, and my family could not in any way be considered rich, but like many people of ambition, he assumed the orthodoxy of the ruling class. "The poor were
born that way," he said. "This is the way they want to live."

By 1984, El Salvador was in the midst of a ferocious civil war (the poor
didn't want to live that way, after all). I was in my early twenties, a college
dropout, and certain of only one thing: I wanted to be a writer. El Salvador and
the war would become my university, and a revolutionary writer named
Salvador Juárez became the dean of my school of poetry – and exile.

I met him at the actual University of El Salvador. At the time, it was barely
functioning as an institution of higher learning. In 1980, the military had staged
a violent occupation of the campus, killing several students and generally doing
what the military does best: destroying everything it could, including smash-
ing all the office equipment and burning books. Because most of the class-
rooms were uninhabitable, lectures were held under shade trees. There were
no textbooks: Professors taught from memory. I came to the campus looking
for writers. I asked the librarian if there were any poets to be found. She mat-
ter-of-factly replied that there happened to be a literary workshop in progress
at that very moment. She pointed to a bombed-out building across the green.

I arrived to find Salvador Juárez holding court. In his early forties, Juárez
was every inch a poet, speaking in mystical whispers, and a master of the
bohemian persona: a revolutionary, a visionary, an alcoholic just as likely to be
found in the wee hours imbibing rotgut with the homeless as at home, playing
the loving husband and father. In his larger-than-life persona, Salvador was following in the footsteps of El Salvador's great twentieth-century bard, Roque
Dalton, a fiery poet and activist who led a peripatetic existence one step ahead

of the authorities. (Of the many legends about Dalton, one of the most famous holds that he was once captured by the government forces, imprisoned, and sentenced to death; at dawn on the day of his scheduled execution, a powerful earthquake made rubble of the prison walls and he waltzed into freedom.)

For a few years, I was Salvador's disciple, following him on a serpentine path of exile to homecoming to exile. He was almost always on a government hit list, and his family begged him to stay out of the country, but after a drinking binge in Mexico City (where many Salvadorans found refuge during the civil war), he'd somehow sneak his way back in.

Salvador patiently mentored me in the ways of poetry. Your lines are too long, he would tell me. Who do you think you are, Whitman? I dutifully shortened them. He also taught me about drinking and generally messing up your life the way I then thought artists were supposed to. What I – a twenty-four-year-old middle-class kid from L.A. – could not fathom back then was that Salvador wasn't drinking because he was a poet. In fact, he'd quit drinking several years earlier. It was the pain of separation from his family and homeland that drove him to despair and to the bottle again. I only began to understand this as I grew older, and I spent more and more time with people traumatized by exile and imprisonment and torture, by dead-end poverty and the pain of forced migrations. Indeed, as a young man, I thought that Salvador's life was a grand adventure, to be read – or written – like a novel. Exile as melodrama.

I haven't heard from Salvador Juárez in many years. But I know that he is in El Salvador with his family. I did hear from a mutual friend that he'd quit drinking, again. The war is over, after all; the guns of the death squads have been silenced. And I also know that the scars from those two decades of ducking and hiding from an implacable enemy – one that wanted him dead only for the stanzas he composed – must be very tender still. They will never truly heal. Salvador Juárez is "home" only in the geographical sense. In a fundamental way, every Salvadoran of the war generation is an exile, whether living at home or abroad: The civil war laid waste to what once was and can never return. I know of several exiles who returned home after the peace accords were signed in Mexico City in 1993. Virtually all wound up returning to live in the States. Understandably, nostalgia is an irresistible elixir for exiles; it balms their wounds while abroad, but ultimately betrays them. The exiles romanticized their erstwhile homeland just as I had through Salvador's passion. Of course, the country that they returned to was as foreign to them as America had been when they'd first gone into exile.

::

Mahmoud Darwish's adult life has been the story of one migration after another, with stops in, among other locations, Cairo, Beirut, Tunis, Amman, Paris, and Ramallah. Even as his poetry has matured from the quasi-pamphleteering tracts of his youth to mature, visionary lyrics inspired by the likes of García Lorca, he continues to court controversy. In 2000, the Israeli Ministry of Education announced plans to include Darwish's verse in a new "multicultural" curriculum, prompting right-wing fulminations. In the end, then-prime minister Ehud Barak, in a Clintonesque appeasement, announced that Israeli schoolchildren were not yet prepared to deal with the likes of Darwish.

Surely, those opposed to his inclusion in the Israeli curriculum were thinking of Darwish less as poet than as militant: Darwish, symbol of the *intifada*. Darwish, the resistance poet:

Record!
I am an Arab
Employed with fellow workers at a quarry
I have eight children
I get them bread
Garments and books
From the rocks . . . ,

I do not supplicate charity at your doors
Nor do I belittle myself at the footsteps of your chamber
So will you be angry?
  – "Identity Card"

Here, in what is probably Darwish's most famous poem, metaphor is shorn in favor of assuming a seething collective voice – the only kind of public voice available in an occupied land where politics in the legal sense is essentially prohibited. It is the cry of an anguished and angry young man (the poem was written in 1964, when Darwish was in his early twenties), the self-same righteous rage one can imagine seizing the mind of a village boy and making him capable of hurling a stone against a soldier armed with an automatic rifle – or even of offering himself as a martyr.

After indulging the direct language of resistance poetry in his youth, Darwish chose to let his imagination run wild, pursuing a Palestinian equivalent of García Lorca's *duende*, an aesthetic ideal that invokes vision from an esoteric source (in Spanish, "duende" refers to a kind of daemonic being that inhabits the achaotic and sublime world of pure spirit). This dramatic shift did not sit well with his more militant comrades in the resistance movement, but it did not essentially shift Darwish's thematic foundation, either. In his lyric imagination, the Occupation and exile remain the pillars of his narratives and existential ruminations.

And I stumbled onto myself
Next to a snake
On a caravan journey,
And I couldn't complete anything
But my ghost.
The land expelled me from itself.
My name pings against my steps like a horseshoe.

> Come closer –
> Let me shuffle along in your name for a while,
> From my void to your eternity,
> O Gilgamesh!
>   – "The Well"

This is the poetics of exile, the soul cleaved by the distance between past and present, between the self of homeland and the banished self wandering the roads ever seeking to return. In his later work, Darwish often directly references *The Epic of Gilgamesh*, the Middle East's foundational literary text (written some 4,000 years ago), itself a story of constant longing and migration: Gilgamesh, one-third man and two-thirds god, searches ceaselessly for a way to circumnavigate mortality only to find that the eternal is achieved only by passing through death's doorway. For Darwish, exile itself is a kind of death:

> I'm the Adam of two Edens lost to me twice.
> Expel me slowly. Kill me slowly
>
> With García Lorca
> Under my olive tree.
>   – "Eleven Planets in the Last Andalusian Sky"

The anguish of two paradises lost: Eden and Palestine. And yet the poet is not dead, since he writes these verses to us from the living death of Limbo, grieving the casualties of exile: space (as in place – the living room of his house in the old village, the contours of the erstwhile nation's boundaries), time (historical, as well as one's own past) and language (how can one speak without a past?). There is no existence without space, time, and language: Exile bequeaths nothingness. And yet Darwish seems to posit that exile can also be a kind of ecstatic state of being, with visions from the proscribed past, the hellish present, and the longed-for future colliding with one another to form, in Darwish's case, a poetic cosmology of pain and desire which is life itself; rootless, the imagination knows no bounds. So kill the poet to resurrect him. Gilgamesh must die for his name to be remembered and his tale told; perhaps dead Palestine undergoes the pangs of her rebirth even now, in the act of her resistance.

> Since the day you were expelled from Paradise a second time
> Our whole world changed,
> Our voices changed,
> Even the greeting between us fell
> Echoless, like a button falling on sand.
> Say Good Morning!
> Say anything,
> So that life may grant me its sweet delight.
>   – "Hooriyya's Teaching"

The very act of remembering, of building one's narrative through language, is existential resistance, the blood of life in the land of the banished. Memory reconstructs time and space, spills into being as language and even more, through Darwish's lyric alchemy, into poetry, a public music that contributes to political resistance, to the possibility of a new Palestine and, as Darwish by all accounts sincerely wishes, to peaceful coexistence with Israel.

There is another kind of resistance poetry, one made not of verses but of the simple, quotidian acts of anyone forced to live far from one's homeland. There are many of these scenes in *The New Americans*. Like Naima Saadeh kneeling to pray in her Chicago apartment, refusing to give in to her husband Hatem's liberal American secularism. Or, also in Chicago, Nigerian refugee Israel Nwidor, sucking up the last of his energy after another grinding day of work in the hotel restaurant to attend a local meeting of fellow exiles seeking redress of the economic and environmental devastation in the homeland. Or future Silicon Valley computer programmer Anjan Bacchu insisting on a traditional wedding back home in India, even as America beckons him with a coveted work visa.

By and large, this is most people's experience of globalization. Call it global exile. It is an epic and painful pilgrimage, not unlike Darwish's or Salvador's or Gilgamesh's, a search not only for survival but for a future that ensures social mobility, the family unit's version of eternity. It is also the struggle to maintain one's own sense of place in a world where addresses are rewritten constantly by an economy that knows no frontiers. In this context, home is less an actual thing than a metaphysical construct: its place is no longer the landscape but the realm of the imaginary. The poets of exile — not to mention immigrants like Hatem and Naima — are bringing a new world into being. They are building a home out of nothing, carving history out of air.

2 :: **Nigeria to Chicago** ::

Israel and Ngozi Nwidor, and Barine Wiwa-Lawani

Barine Wiwa-Lawani

The boughs are broken, an earthquake
Rides upon the sway of chants, a flood
Unseasonal, a power of invocations.
Meander how it will, the river
Ends in lakes, in seas, in the ocean's
Savage waves. Our Flood's alluvial paths
Will spring the shrunken seeds;
Rains
Shall cleanse the leaves of blood.

—Wole Soyinka, *Ogun Aibimañ*

It's always hard
To leave your country
You leave
Your mother and father
You leave
Your motherland
A land you are proud of . . .

—Hussein Affey, Somali refugee living in Chicago for twenty-five years

::

THE REFUGEE CAMP IN THE WEST AFRICAN NATION OF BENIN IS JUST AS ONE
would imagine such a compound anywhere in the world: row upon row
of canvas tents, people lining up for rations. Heat, dust, and hopeless-
ness. What one rarely imagines is how long people actually live in camps
like these as they wait to escape limbo and carve out a future. The
Nwidor and Wiwa-Lawani families have lived in the camp for over two
years before securing asylum in the United States—two years of waiting
for the achingly slow wheels of the bureaucracy of the office of the

United Nations High Commissioner for Refugees (UNHCR) to turn and resolve their status.

After interminable days of living in a tent, ever sweeping out the dust that blows in off the bare ground outside, sleeping on a mat laid above hardscrabble earth, Israel and Ngozi Nwidor hear their names called by an International Organization of Migration (IOM) caseworker. How they've dreamed of this moment of escape from this virtual prison! Finally, there will be a place to truly rest. Perhaps soon Israel Nwidor will have his first good night's sleep since going into exile. "For three years, I have not known what it is like to lie on a good bed," says Israel. "That first night in America if I could just have a nice sleep on a good bed."

Israel and Ngozi have won political asylum in the United States of America and will soon board a flight to Chicago. For other families departing the refugee camp, the destinations include California, New York, Georgia, and Iowa. Israel and Ngozi are elated, of course, but it is also a bittersweet moment. They fled Ogoniland, their native community on the Niger Delta, after deadly political violence over the exploitation of rich oil deposits in their homeland. With thousands of other Ogoni, they crossed the border into neighboring Benin as refugees. During their long sojourn there, they held on to the hope that somehow the situation would turn for the better back home and allow them to return. With their passage to America, it seems, they are truly leaving Ogoniland for good. It is the first time, not counting their flight into Benin, they have been away from Nigeria.

The IOM caseworker also calls Barine Wiwa-Lawani, sister of famed, and martyred, Ogoni writer-activist Ken Saro-Wiwa. Saro-Wiwa's execution along with eight other leaders of the Movement for the Survival of the Ogoni People (MOSOP) by the brutal Nigerian military regime of General Sani Abacha was the final atrocity that compelled the flight of thousands of Ogoni into Benin. Because of her slain brother and her own standing in the Ogoni community as a successful entrepreneur, Barine was afforded great respect and affection by her fellow refugees. She'd suffered as much or more than the others. The government bulldozed her two restaurants and catering school; she was forced to flee for her life. Not long after arriving at the refugee camp, tragedy struck again: She received word that her husband had succumbed to cancer in England. The Ogoni in the Benin camp insisted that she and her three children take one of the few rooms available in an abandoned hospital on whose property the camp was situated, rather than one of the hundreds of tents most of the refugees live in. Her family has lived in the relative comfort of cramped rooms of unfinished concrete for the last two years. Barine stands out in the camp. She wears fashionable dresses and headscarves that set her apart. She studied in England and has visited Paris, Amsterdam, and other points abroad, and so the impending trip to America is not quite as momentous—and unsettling—an occasion as it is for the others. Barine fully expects that with her entrepreneurial experience, she will find a way to make a decent living in America. "I've been used to traveling," she says. "I'll find a way to manage."

Israel Nwidor has high expectations as well. In Nigeria, he studied petrochemical engineering—hoping for a job within the very oil industry that spawned the political crisis which sent the Ogoni into exile. (He hoped to use his skills to address the environmental impact of oil exploitation in Ogoniland.) But most likely because of his ethnicity, Israel had been unable to secure a job in the industry and had worked as a high school science teacher.

But now Barine and the Nwidors are refugees, and though they don't know it yet, it's as if their past lives—including work experience—have been erased by history as suddenly as a machete slicing through a coconut. Decades of good faith diplomatic efforts to humanize the politics of refugee status (the United Nations created the UNHCR over half a century ago) have not altered the reality that refugees are most often treated paternalistically by their host countries. They are perceived as victims, and they are treated as such. In the popular consciousness, the very word "refugee" brings to mind impoverished, passive victims of brutality—nameless peasants, not restaurateurs or petrochemical engineers. Israel will not work as an engineer in America. Barine will not own a restaurant or even be a chef—at least not at first. The expectations of the adopted country's "hosts" are low, because it is impossible for the American middle-class to imagine a Third World middle-class victim. Perhaps they cannot imagine a Third World middle-class at all.

It is not that Barine Wiwa-Lawani and the Nwidors are not victims. Barine lost her brother Ken when a military kangaroo court ordered and the state carried out his execution. Israel was captured and beaten by soldiers, taking a daily ration of a dozen searing lashes on his back from thick electrical cables for four months before he escaped into the bush. Ngozi recalls arriving at school one day only to have classmates whisper that the army had come asking for her. Entire Ogoni villages were razed under General Abacha's reign of terror; much Ogoni blood was spilled, like the oil bleeding from the wounds of the earth occasioned by the exploitation of multinational corporations like Shell International Petroleum Company.

But the Ogoni were not passive victims in any way. After all, it was their activism against the environmental degradation and economic exploitation of their homeland that provoked the violent response from the government—with the blessing, if not the abetting, of the oil companies, according to sources like Human Rights Watch. Theirs was a tight-knit grassroots movement, a challenge to Nigeria's antidemocratic history since independence (there has been scarcely more than a decade's worth of civilian rule in the country since 1960). As such, the Ogoni merit the title of freedom fighters—but the U.S. government usually

COURTESY ISRAEL AND NGOZI NWIDOR / KARTEMQUIN FILMS

Israel and Ngozi Nwidor in Nigeria, 1988

reserves this moniker for anticommunist brigades that invariably wind up on Amnesty International's list of human-rights abusers.

Indeed, U.S. refugee policy—which was not actually codified until passage of the Refugee Act of 1980, largely in response to the Vietnamese exodus after the fall of Saigon—closely followed the contours of the Cold

War. We embraced people fleeing Communist regimes and turned away those we deemed Communist (whom we defined as anyone from Maoists to social democratic reformers and occasionally even Christian Democrats). Presidents Reagan and Bush used the language of the Refugee Act (a prospective entrant had to prove a "well-founded fear of persecution" in the homeland) to opportunistically distinguish between "political" and "economic" refugees. In the 1980s, during the civil wars in Central America, most Nicaraguans claiming persecution under the Sandinista regime were admitted under the act; 98 percent of Salvadorans and Guatemalans, who fled right-wing (and U.S.-backed) repression, were not. Refugee advocates sued the federal government in *American Baptist Churches v. Thornburgh* in 1991 and won temporary legal residency (which continues to be granted) for millions who'd fled the violence.

But who is and isn't recognized as a refugee remains a highly politicized issue. To this day, Cubans who make it onto the beach in Florida are granted automatic asylum; Haitians and Dominicans, who endured brutal regimes backed by the U.S. through much of the twentieth century, have not received the same treatment. In the end, the distinction of whether one is a political or economic refugee owes everything to political expediency and not humanitarian concerns.

The UNHCR reports that there were 14.5 million refugees worldwide in 2001, one million more than there were the previous year. There were also between 20 and 24 million people who had been "internally displaced" within the borders of their own countries—a significant number of these will eventually migrate beyond them. An average of 15,000 people around the world are forced to flee their homes every day. Despite the increase in numbers, funding for the UNHCR has declined; the organization faces a shortfall of $100 million and has been forced to lay off some 700 employees. The United States of America is the single largest donor-nation to the UN refugee fund. In its FY2002 budget, the

Bush administration proposed cutting U.S. support by $5 million. Accounting for inflation, the U.S. has scaled back its commitment to the refugee cause by nearly $57 million in the last five years.

So there is the way the Ogoni perceive themselves and the way they are perceived by others with their status as "refugees." It is not that they do not encounter kindness in the hearts of strangers—there are people willing to help at every turn. But even among "liberals" of generous heart there is often a hint of condescension, as if the gesture of generosity revealed more about the giver's need to give than the receiver's need to receive.

::

Israel Nwidor has a beaming moon of a face. He's a gregarious and optimistic sort, and his vision of America is nothing if not optimistic. He says that he is happy to be going to a northern city like Chicago. "Blacks in the northern part of America are free," he says. "They are not discriminated against like those in the South. But I think as an immigrant moving to America and being in the northern part of America that I'll be treated like any other black man in the northern part of America."

Israel's wife Ngozi is more reticent. She is thin, almost gaunt, and her plaintive look shows the scars of the last three years as clearly as Israel's hides them. "I've never been to America," she says, with an air of resignation, "but when I go there, I will do as the others do."

Israel echoes the thought, with his usual enthusiasm. "When I read novels about America, I read about hamburgers. I don't even know what a hamburger is, but I will go there and I will learn and I will eat them.

The occasion of Barine's and the Nwidors' departure from the camp is both a joyous and poignant affair. Everyone gathers around the bus that will ferry the lucky few refugees who've gained asylum to the airport and on to their new homes in America. The Anglophone Ogoni break out in a song penned by one of the musicians in the camp:

No one wants to be a refugee in his lifetime
Some run away to Cameroon . . . for freedom
Some run away to Republic of Ghana . . . for asylum

And they chant their old tribal slogan: Ogoni, Great People! Ogoni, Great People! Israel's close friend, Ikobari Senewa, a leader in MOSOP, pulls him aside to give him some final words of inspiration. "Today, when you leave here and enter that bus and go to the airport, be determined and be ready to work," says Israel's pastor. Israel listens intently with his head bowed. "If you don't succeed, the Ogoni have failed because your success is your family's success, it is your village's success, it is the success of the Ogoni. If you fail, it is a family failure, it is an Ogoni failure, we have all failed. May the Lord be with you as you go."

Israel nods his head, fully aware of the weight on his shoulders, but also buoyed by the fresh energy his imminent departure from the camp surely gives him. As he prepares to board the bus (bearing the name Les Rapides de l'Albatross, which may or may not be prophetic), he imagines America—how else?—cinematically.

"Now as I'm going to America, I think I'm just like Eddie Murphy in *Coming to America*," he says, without a trace of irony—indeed, for Israel the film is more like an inspirational epic.

Now Israel climbs the first step on to the bus, and turns around to give one last look at his people, who break into song anew, this time, fittingly, with an emotional rendition of "We Shall Overcome."

::

The Ogoni struggle became international news in the mid-1990s, achieving a level of radical chic such that even corporations like The Body Shop pledged support to the movement. But the media attention and solidarity did not alter a seemingly predestined tragic course of events, culminating with the deaths not just of Ken Saro-Wiwa and his MOSOP cohort (eight were executed along with him), but of hundreds of Ogonis, with thousands more tossed into exile.

The Ogoni story unfolds chiefly from the discovery of rich oil deposits in the Niger Delta in 1955. Foreign companies arrived to exploit the black gold and with promises of a better life not just for Delta people like the Ogoni but for all Nigerians. Among the transnationals, Shell was the strongest presence, eventually coming to produce about half of Nigeria's crude. The country did not win independence from Great Britain until 1960; the exploitation of oil resources thus is rooted in the colonial past and continues in the neocolonial present.

The promises of a better life have by and large been unfulfilled by the multinationals that have contracted with Nigeria's post-independence regimes—mostly military dictatorships. While those Nigerians who have jobs with the oil companies can earn generous salaries, the vast majority of those in the oil-producing regions remain un- or underemployed. In any case, much of the vast wealth produced by the industry—Nigeria produces up to 22 billion barrels of crude annually, processing some 2 million barrels a day—evaporates with government mismanagement or is siphoned into offshore accounts by avaricious native leaders rather than being invested in critical community infrastructure. Shell's Nigeria operation is worth some $14 billion (its parent, Shell International Petroleum Company, rakes in $300 billion a year). By comparison, the Nigerian government's annual budget is $30 billion. Meanwhile, the average Nigerian laborer can expect to earn $260 a year.

Barine in Bane, Nigeria

In an investigative report published in Britain's *Guardian* newspaper, journalist John Vidal highlights the disparity between those few Nigerians who've been favored by the oil economy and the majority who haven't. He visits two health clinics, both run by Shell. One, in Ogoniland, is a community clinic (set up in the spirit of "reconciliation" with the Ogoni in the wake of the deadly conflict). The other is for company employees in Port Harcourt. At the community center, there is no glass in the windows of the men's ward, there are birds' nest in the hallways, and surgery is performed only once a week, if at all, depending on whether the surgeon decides to make the trip. Port Harcourt is only twenty-five miles away, but it might as well be across the Atlantic or in London, the old metropole. Specifically built to treat Shell's own employees, the company has spent an estimated $25 million dollars for its state-of-the-art facility, which includes emergency and maternity wards and a kitchen staff of seven.

For its part, Shell claims that it is spending tens of millions of dollars in social projects precisely in communities such as Ogoniland. But grassroots leaders reply that Shell is ill-equipped to oversee community-development projects and that its performance is, at best, paternalistic and poorly organized. Another part of the problem, activists say, is local corruption. Funds may arrive in a village to pay for a new roof on the school; months later the roof will still be leaking, but a tribal chief may be showing off the new roof to his house.

Corruption is a perennial theme in the postcolonial setting. Seen from the perspective of the First World—through a tourist's eyes, let's say—the problem seems to be a lack of ethics or some sort of "cultural" phenomenon. But such a worldview presupposes a Western democratic–style social contract that clearly demarcates what is acceptable behavior and what is not. Colonialism destroyed the primordial social contracts of its subject nations and did little to help rebuild them after independence. Corruption, therefore, cannot be divorced from colonial history. It is the very continuation of it by other means—most pathetically, by "native" preying upon "native."

In this context, the arrival of multinational corporations to former colonies across the globe brings the macabre ghosts of history back to life.

The *Guardian*'s Vidal quotes a local Ogoni leader:

"It would have been better if oil had never come. At least then we would not have the pollution, the destitution and the sorrow.

"We have been denied everything and in return we have had our lands and sky, rivers and fields polluted. We have been repressed, killed and tortured and now we are told there is no hope for us to develop. Do you wonder why we are angry?"

::

The wetlands of the Niger Delta are the largest such region in Africa and among the biggest in the world. Some 6,000 miles of oil pipelines meander through the wetlands, and much of the piping is in deteriorated condition. Spills large and small leak oil onto farmland and into aquifers that provide water to local populations. Gas "flaring" tosses pollutants into the air, and careless effluent discharges lay waste to the land. Airborne pollution causes acid rain, to the extent of corroding the aluminum roofing of Ogoni houses. The oil economy has had an impact on practically every aspect of the wetlands' fragile ecosystem.

"Every day the people take in these gases," says Israel Nwidor. "The air is polluted. All [of Shell's] pipelines are exposed, they are not buried, crude oil passing through [them]. We used to fish very well, but the fish died off. The farmland, you cannot plant. You cannot control your own economy. You cannot have anything of what God has given to you. These were the things that really touched the minds of the Ogonis. And we decided to form this nonviolent organization."

That the Movement for the Survival of the Ogoni People chose the nonviolent path toward change in the style of the American Civil Rights Movement (which itself was inspired by Gandhi's nonviolent struggle against colonialism) is no coincidence. Among Ken Saro-Wiwa's personal pantheon of heroes were the Rev. Martin Luther King Jr. and Mahatma Gandhi.

The Ogoni bear the status of "minority ethnic group" in Nigeria. Their numbers pale in comparison to the Igbo of the eastern lands, the Yoruba of the west, and the Hausa-Fulani—the Muslim peoples of the north. The Ogoni are some half a million strong, but are among the smallest ethnicities amid the staggering diversity of Nigerian society— there are 250 ethnic groups in the country. Nigeria, the modern federation of these nations-within-a-nation, is the product solely of the colonial imagination, the "scramble" for, and "partition" of African lands in the late nineteenth and early twentieth centuries. Each European power extended its dominion as far as it could, usually without regard for aboriginal boundaries. The English made the Lower Niger region an Anglophone protectorate; but for the British grab, it would be very unlikely that the Yoruba, Igbo, Hausa-Fulani, and Ogoni would live in the same "nation" today.

Ogoniland just happens to sit in the heart of the oil-rich Niger Delta. The Ogoni of antiquity did not know this, of course. Modernity brought with it not just the English, the English language, and second-class citizenship—it also sowed the seeds of conflicts that are still very much alive today. Indeed, the oil deposits of the Delta were a source of contention long before the creation of MOSOP in 1991. Soon after independence, rivalries among the majority ethnic groups—rifts that had been exploited by the British in classic colonial "divide and conquer" fashion—ignited the Biafran War. Among the reasons for the conflict, control of the Delta oil fields was paramount.

Oil was discovered in Ogoniland in 1958, and its exploitation began shortly thereafter. But over three decades later at the end of 1980s, the Ogoni lived much the same way they had before Shell arrived. Ogoni villages were collections of mud huts, with a scarcity of electricity and water infrastructure. Health and educational resources were underfunded and poorly staffed. In many ways, conditions had worsened over the years, despite continued promises from the government and the multinationals about a prosperous future. Environmental degradation from oil exploitation threatened fisherman and small farmers, the lifeblood of the Ogoni. Once considered the breadbasket of the region, Ogoniland's farms yielded less and the Ogoni, long a self-sufficient people, now saw it necessary to import foodstuffs.

Ken Saro-Wiwa, an Ogoni writer with a longtime interest in politics, began documenting not only the degradation of his homeland, but also what he called the political and corporate "lootocracy" of Nigeria as whole. In regular newspaper columns, via a TV sitcom that he created, and in some 25 volumes of novels, plays, poetry, and children's literature, Saro-Wiwa became easily the most important Ogoni public figure of his time. A charismatic personality—part egotist and part visionary, as he is described by his son Ken Wiwa in the tender and evocative memoir *In the Shadow of a Saint*—Saro-Wiwa was one of the major forces behind the founding of MOSOP, which was christened with the publication of the "Ogoni Bill of Rights," authored by Saro-Wiwa himself. The document called for the federal government to recognize the Ogoni right to political autonomy, to protection from environmental degradation, to religious freedom, and to the development of Ogoni languages and culture.

Ken Saro-Wiwa, the pipe-smoking intellectual with gregarious manner and larger-than-life persona (despite standing a mere five-foot-one!), was named MOSOP's publicity chief. The organization presented its founding document to the military government of General Ibrahim Babandgida, which ignored it. But after two years of diligent organizing spearheaded by Ken Saro-Wiwa's tireless touring of the Ogoni region to drum up support for the cause, MOSOP sprang to life like fire from glowing embers. On January 4, 1993, declared by the United Nations as the official beginning of the International Year for the World's Indigenous

Populations, MOSOP held its first mass rally. "The cream of Ogoni society was present and the atmosphere was euphoric . . . drummers thumped away and dance troupes performed," wrote Saro-Wiwa later from prison in *A Month and A Day: A Detention Diary*. Speeches were declaimed and received with unanimous acclaim. "I knew that a new seed had germinated and everything would have to be done to water, nurture, grow and harvest it. Ogoni would surely not be the same again."

In his own speech to the assembly, Saro-Wiwa spontaneously named Shell persona non grata in Ogoniland. It was truly the baptism of MOSOP—which would garner frequent international press in the ensuing years—and, with his David-against-Goliath declaration, it is quite probable that Ken Saro-Wiwa sealed his fate on that very day. He would be hanged barely three years later.

::

It could be said that the late nineteenth and early twentieth centuries, when colonial empires were at their height in Africa and the Asian subcontinent, were a kind of precursor to what we today call globalization. To "pacify" native populations and exploit resources and labor, European powers had a vast arsenal at their disposal, including military might, the merchant class, and missionary churches. Commerce and culture flowed between colony and metropole, and the tide was decidedly in favor of the latter. But the empires, for better and for worse, left their cultural residue in the colonies as well, in the form of language, dress, food, music.

The middle-class experience of globalization is not unlike the relation between colony and metropole. Once, tobaccos, coffees, and teas were the novelty; today, it can be a tattoo design, a "primitive" beat, or spiritual tradition. And, as in colonialism, the merchant class—now multi-nationalized—is at the vanguard of the flow, working toward its bottom line in tandem with regional state apparati that get their share of the pie, too—as long as they ensure a "favorable business climate." This is the dark side of globalization. In practice, it can mean repression as savage as that during the colonial era. The global middle class, by and large, turns away from such unseemly matters and goes on enjoying the fruits of the transaction. (At most, global moguls like Kathy Lee Gifford shed crocodile tears over the treatment of workers in the Third World sweatshops that stitch together their jeans.)

Ken Saro-Wiwa saw the relationship between successive Nigerian regimes and the multinational companies for what it was. In the case of the Ogoni conflict, there is ample evidence to suggest complicity between Shell and the Nigerian federal government in the tragic outcome of events, including Saro-Wiwa's execution. Only a few months after the mass MOSOP rally, Shell, after a respite in operations because of the political turbulence, decided to resume work in Ogoniland. While working on a major pipeline, it requested protection from the Nigerian government, which promptly offered the services of its military. The result: Soldiers fired upon unarmed civilians and the first Ogoni victim of the conflict received a bullet in the back.

The government, for its part, drafted legislation that prohibited anyone to utter the term "political autonomy," effectively turning MOSOP into an outlaw organization. Ken Wiwa notes in *In the Shadow of a Saint* that in the wake of the passage of the "Treason and Treasonable Felony Decree," as it was called, Shell "coincidentally" emitted a press release accusing his father of attempting to establish "political self-determination" for the Ogoni. In short, it was as if Shell were serving as jury for a Nigerian kangaroo court.

The remainder of 1993 saw dozens of clashes in Ogoniland, with a death toll rising into the hundreds. While the government regularly blamed "ethnic clashes" (a convenient excuse in Nigeria), MOSOP claimed that the government and Shell were the culprits. When General Sani Abacha took power in a coup, he made it a priority to quell the unrest in Ogoniland. His methods to this end were typical: to bribe, humiliate, brutalize, terrorize, and to turn brother against brother.

In early 1994, Abacha created a machinery of repression called the Rivers State Internal Security (RSIS). One of the RSIS's first acts was a massacre of over 800 Ogoni, leaving the villages themselves in smoking ruins. Meanwhile, internal divisions among the Ogoni were exacerbated by paranoia and government manipulation; vigilante violence was not uncommon. During this period, Ken Saro-Wiwa was arrested and detained three times; the third occasion was his last. He was accused of masterminding the murder of several Ogoni chiefs, and he was convicted and sentenced by a tribunal receiving its orders directly from the government.

Ken Saro-Wiwa and thousands of other Ogonis died because General Sani Abacha was trying to show Shell that the government was firmly in control—that the coast was clear to resume operations in Ogoniland. It was as if the general were trading blood for oil. General Abacha died suddenly in 1998; yet another military man, President Olusegun Obasanjo, was elected democratically in 1999. In the three years following, some 10,000 Nigerians were killed in sectarian violence. Shell Nigeria has yet to resume operations in Ogoniland, and MOSOP continues to press its cause.

::

It is a testament to the unique power of the Hollywood image that to this day many immigrants are shocked to discover that in America there is poverty, violence, and discrimination. The Land of the Free is part of the real world, after all.

Israel and Ngozi did not expect instant riches when they arrived in Chicago, but they didn't expect to work as steward and housekeeper, respectively, in two downtown hotels. When Israel departed the refugee camp in Benin, he said that he felt like Eddie Murphy in *Coming to America*. Now, he is playing the role: scrubbing the grease off a huge oven in the Hyatt Hotel kitchen in the wee hours. Meanwhile, Ngozi pushes her cart from room to room in the Fairmont Hotel, knocking on doors, and calling out "housekeeping!" and dealing with the indignities that only housekeepers know. Israel and Ngozi both make $7 an hour.

It is not that Israel and Ngozi aren't willing to work hard. But Israel quickly discovered that his petrochemical engineering degree was useless in the States, and Ngozi realized that her goal of becoming a nurse would mean juggling school, work, and tending to her two young children. So work hard they do, but their pride is wounded by the quotidian humiliations of being an immigrant in America: At every turn, it seems, there are attitudes of condescension or outright bigotry. As a black man, Israel bears the brunt of it. A nerdish, bespectacled supervisor at the hotel tells us that he thinks "intellectual people" like Israel are "great, because they're always thinking, thinking ahead and knowing, 'Okay, we have a function for 2,200 people, what do we need to do?" He adds that he has several immigrant employees on staff that are "veterinarians and doctors." On another occasion, a different supervisor conducts a training session in the hotel kitchen. The supervisor is white, almost all the employees black, Asian, or Hispanic; most are immigrants. He asks the men to get down on their knees to inspect the space beneath a counter. "Come on, if I can get down, you can, too," he says. Most of the men comply. Israel only bends halfway down. The supervisor barks rhetorically, "Clean or dirty?" like a drill sergeant, and the men follow his cue: "Dirty!" they chorus.

My hometown of Los Angeles received some 500,000 Central American refugees during the 1980s as a result of the civil wars in El Salvador, Guatemala, and Nicaragua. The violence cut across class lines; peasant and lawyer alike found themselves on the rough streets of the Pico-Union district, the portal for new arrivals. On more occasions than I can count, I'd strike up a conversation with a waiter, store clerk, street vendor, day laborer, or homeless drunk, and hear the story of how a doctorate in literature, a law degree, a medical practice, thirty years of business experience, or a government post back home meant nothing in America. The past was just that: Their lives and livelihoods were irretrievable, as were their social status and reputations. These men and women had the same names and bodies as they did back home, but a mistake had been made when they arrived in America: Somehow, they were no longer themselves, their pride and sometimes even their desire torn from them like a drug suspect stripped naked.

It is a steep learning curve for the Nwidors. An African refugee caseworker offers a workshop for new immigrants on the basics of life in an American city. "In Africa, someone knocking, you say come on in," he says. "Here, you have to know who that person is." He then explains the function of a peephole. "You say, who's knocking on my door, and if they don't say, you don't open to them!"

Even the simple facts of life that most Americans take for granted are tough to translate. Like ATM cards, for instance. When another caseworker instructs them how to access their public aid payments (which refugees receive for their first six months in the U.S.), Israel and Ngozi are baffled by the need for a secret PIN number. They try to show it to a caseworker over and over again, while she keeps telling them to keep it to themselves.

One of the toughest lessons of all for Israel comes when he commits a typically American crime, known to African Americans as a DWB— Driving While Black. While carpooling to the hotel with a Vietnamese co-worker, four police cruisers converged on them at once and pull them over. The officer proceeded to search the car and the men for drugs.

"I could not believe it," Israel says, astonished and seething. "The police officer was insulting us, using all kind of foul languages—'Fuck you'—a police officer! I was amazed. I was so mad, I went straight up to him and said that I feel that he did this because he found out we are immigrants."

Still, Israel's optimism is nearly indefatigable. The "north of America" may not be as hospitable to black men as he thought back in Africa, but he still does his best to acclimate. He's bought a few country music tapes that he plays loudly in his car. He knows the lyrics to a George Strait number. With the window rolled down and George's and Israel's voices harmonizing, this can cause some head-turning among white Americans, but Israel goes on "doing as they do."

::

Barine Wiwa-Lawani is having to lower expectations for the moment as well. She is a cosmopolitan woman with a degree in hotel management from a British university. As such, she is not unlike most other African immigrants to the United States—between 1970 and 1990, 96 percent of the Nigerians who arrived here had college degrees. But Barine quickly discovers that she will not enter the job market at anywhere near her level. She applies for a position at one hotel, and her résumé clearly intimidates. "Someone like you, with a degree and academic background, how are you going to feel having me tell you what to do?" she is told.

So she hides away the cosmopolitan, academic Barine and takes a

Barine at work

position as an "assistant chef," a sexy term for someone who chops veggies and washes meat before it's cooked. "Most of the time I behave as if I'm a fool and I don't know anything," she says. She soon becomes aware that she will have to take on more work if she is going to be able to support her four children as a single mom. Ultimately, she juggles three "assistant chef" positions to make ends meet. It is impossible not to think of home. In Nigeria, she ran a restaurant and a cooking school. The restaurant was literally bulldozed by the government forces during the violence in Ogoniland. The place was called Zinu's.

In her spare time—it's hard to imagine she has any—she takes a computer course and doodles with a design program, creating a menu for a restaurant that doesn't exist. She hopes to open a restaurant again one day—she will still call it Zinu's, and it will still be African cuisine—but she just doesn't know where. She is counting on the wheels of history turning in Nigeria; she imagines herself back in the homeland one day. And soon after she arrives in Chicago, they do turn—a civilian government is elected with promises of respect for human rights. But Barine knows that there are no guarantees in a country with a political climate like Nigeria's, where the violence, like promises of peace, comes as suddenly as an afternoon thunderstorm and evaporates just as quickly. It is the way politics works in most of the world these days. And as ambitious as her career goals are, she must also deal with the fact that she is a single mother to four children.

::

The experience of the children of immigrants is altogether different than that of their parents. If they arrive in the adopted country very young, their recollections of the homeland tend to dissipate quickly and thus they are able to adapt faster than their parents. But if they arrive as teenagers, the typical alienation of their age group can combine with the alienation of their immigrant-ness to create an intolerable tension that can lead to depression or volatile behavior. Barine's two youngest daughters, fifteen-year-old fraternal twins Zina and Nini, fall into the latter group.

Zina and Nini attend Sullivan High in the Rogers Park neighborhood of Chicago. It takes them some getting used to walking through metal detectors and past security guards; Nigeria may have political violence, but not school violence. At first, the girls comport themselves with an almost impenetrable shyness. A guidance counselor comes up with the idea of introducing them to a fellow Nigerian student, but the kid has lived in the U.S. for years and belongs to another one of Nigeria's 250 ethnic groups. The twins have nothing at all in common with the boy.

Later, the girls attend an after-school program apparently aimed at teens from underprivileged backgrounds who rarely have access to typical middle-class American public rituals such as museums and restaurants. Program leader Ginger Spitzer, a white woman, has her hands full with the multiethnic crew. She instructs them in etiquette in preparation for a field trip to the Red Lobster. After going over the basics—don't announce to the entire restaurant that your fork is dirty or that so-and-so is eating like a pig—she asks the students if there's anything that irks them when they eat in public. Immediately, one of the African American teens complains about people who speak "their own language," setting up a classic African vs. African American tension and painfully placing Nini and Zina in the role of outsiders—as if they weren't already. Ginger is placed in the curious position of a white woman playing intermediary between the two. For the moment, she sides with the non-immigrants.

"One of the things you don't want to do is [to] speak Spanish—"

An African American student interjects: "Or Nigerian!" (Which, of course, is not a language.)

"Yeah, or any language," Ginger continues.

To which Nini bravely retorts: "I speak English!"

"Yes, of course you do," Ginger condescends, and concludes: "It's no different than me whispering."

Setting aside the issue of etiquette in the age of globalization and whether or not speaking in a "foreign" tongue in a public space such as a restaurant is indeed akin to "whispering," can there be much doubt about the impact of such opinions when they are heaved upon immigrant kids like Zina and Nini? Millions of Latino kids in the Southwestern United States were routinely reprimanded for speaking Spanish in public spaces such as schools. I have many friends who attended parochial schools in the 1950s and 1960s and who are quite probably lapsed Catholics today precisely because the nuns commonly rapped their knuckles with wooden rulers when they were caught speaking their native tongue. You don't often hear of such outright abuse today, but what about the fierce debates over "English Only" laws (which about a dozen states have passed in recent years, in addition to scores, if not hundreds, of municipalities)? Aren't the monolingual activists essentially saying *those people are whispering?* What I'm most curious about is what these activists actually think that the immigrants are saying about them. Such political punishment over issues of culture can have long-lasting effects. The immigrant child is being told that her maternal language is, somehow, less than. That it's not proper, not the lingua franca, but rather an artifact from a time and place far removed from the American present and future. Time to shed your skin. Assimilate. How can a child not internalize this message negatively? It would seem that there are only two responses to the assimilation gauntlet. One, give up the cultural ghost and act "American"—whatever that is—and two, fight against the established order and become an ethnic rebel. It's a Gordian knot: Neither, in the end, is a permanent solution, and neither can be invoked without paying an existential price.

Unfortunately, the culture war in miniature between the twins and their classmates does not end at Sullivan High. On the school bus en route to the Red Lobster, one of Zina's new African American friends— apparently Zina's done better at socializing than her twin—makes fun of Nini's accent.

"She imitated the way I talk," Nini complains to her sister.

Zina now must choose between sticking up for her sister—and risk alienating her fragile connection to the African American kids she's trying to relate to—or betraying her. Peer pressure wins out.

"Does it mean she's making fun of you?" Zina says. "Maybe she likes the accent, too."

The pathetic irony here is that Nini has been trying to imitate the African American accent all along to fit in like her sister.

"[So] don't speak like an American, then," Zina tells her twin, and in doing so, negates herself. "You're trying to speak like an American."

"Don't speak like them???" Nini spits out incredulously. "Don't speak like them??? Do you know how it feels???"

Zina: "Nini, there is nothing there. It's not like they killed you or something."

But of course, for Nini it feels exactly like that: a humiliation made all the more profound by her sister's betrayal. She sits by herself next to the window of the bus, staring out at the incomprehensible bustle of the American streets through the tears in her eyes.

::

"Momma, please sing a special song for me," Israel says.

The old woman smiles and begins singing softly, a melody as old as the Ogoni village.

It is a beautiful moment—but Israel and his mother are not in the same room when it occurs. Israel is in Chicago and his mother is back home in Bane, the Ogoni village from which the Nwidor family hails. Her son speaks to her virtually—via a videotape playing on the TV in her living room.

The distance between Ogoniland and Chicago is roughly 6,000 miles and the time difference is six hours. But those numbers don't come close to capturing the chasm of time and space that separates the Nwidor family when they speak via a phone line that carries their voices across the Atlantic. Or, as is the case in *The New Americans*, when they communicate via a "video letter" shot by the producers of the series.

Israel, Ngozi and children in Chicago

Now it is Ngozi's turn to speak to her relatives, who have gathered at the Nwidors' house for the occasion as well. She tells her mother in Igbo that she is pregnant, and that she needs the recipe for pepper soup. "I've got all the ingredients," mother replies in real time, as if it was an actual conversation with her daughter. "I miss you," Ngozi says, now in tears.

The tears prompt Israel's mother to damn the distance between them. "If you cry like this now, where will you get the tears to cry when I die?" she says bitterly.

Just as immigrant travails in the U.S. generally do not dominate our pop historical narrative (Horatio Alger tales and *The Godfather* do), neither does the emotional trauma produced by distance from the homeland. The pain begins with embarking on the journey to America.

Invariably, there is a tearful embrace with loved ones at an airport or bus station, a moment that is relived time and again during weeks, months, and years of separation from family back home.

Many immigrants carry faded and cracked photographs of loved ones in their wallets and purses. Once, in a North Carolina tobacco field, I watched as several Mexican migrant laborers each carefully took out photos of wives, children, mothers, and fathers. It was quite a sight, to see these erstwhile macho wanderers of the undocumented labor trail—masters of the rough and tumble life of the "illegal alien," always just one step ahead of the *migra* or the local police—suddenly misty-eyed, voices cracking as they held those images as gingerly as one would a newly discovered archeological relic. Those unsmiling faces— Old World family photos are rarely casual affairs like they are in America—were the migrants' only connection to the past, and the only physical reminder of why they'd faced the dangers of the migrant road in the first place.

The technological advances responsible for globalization may be reconcentrating wealth in the hands of a few capitalist globe-trotters, but there has also been a degree of "trickle down" and everything from VCRs and DVD players and cable television to digital cameras and pagers and cell phones have transformed migrant enclaves in the States as well as the social geography of the Old Countries.

When my mother emigrated from El Salvador in 1957, she boarded a Pan American bi-motor and arrived nearly a dozen hours later in San Francisco (the flight today takes about five hours). To speak to her mom and dad and brother and sister back home, she dialed an American long-distance operator who in turned dialed a long-distance operator in San Salvador. In the best of circumstances, one had to shout into the phone to be heard, but after a hurricane or earthquake, phone lines would be down for weeks at a time. Nonetheless, the phone companies needed business, and the immigrants needed desperately to reconnect with loved ones, and on occasion, radio relays were set up along the three-thousand-mile stretch between California and El Salvador. The delays produced a terrible echo that rendered these conversations rather impractical, but time and space had been conquered: "I miss you" and "I love you" were spoken and heard.

In today's migrant world, VHS or digital video is increasingly the preferred "virtual epistolary form." One wonders about the different emotional timbres of writing a letter that will be read in weeks or months, or a real-time, disembodied conversation by phone, and seeing loved ones performing their greetings in corporeal form on a thirteen-inch television screen. Is it something like the difference between reading a novel and watching a film? Between writing a letter and writing an E-mail or having an "instant" conversation via the Internet? The emotional impact is obviously more immediate, in certain cases even overwhelming. Consider this experience from the point of view of the Nwidors in Nigeria: pop a cassette into the VCR and suddenly there is Israel, Ngozi, and their children. Right away, everyone back home notes that Israel's daughter Zobari gained weight. Seen through Israel's mother's eyes, the change has taken place instantaneously: her grandchild gained those fifteen pounds in the blink of an eye—that is, since she last saw her. And the way the granddaughters speak ("Black American English," a relative says back home): how quickly American culture has made them foreign to their own! When Ngozi asks for the pepper soup recipe, the elders back home nod approvingly. At least Ngozi has not forgotten from whence she came!

For many migrant families, such virtual communication is still a novelty. Israel's mother and brother and Ngozi's mother all respond directly to the images of their relatives on the screen, reminding me of those legends about the first showings of "moving pictures" in the Western territories of the States, when gunfighters drew their pistols and shot back at the gunmen represented on the screen. The time and space of modernity clashes with the time and space of the Old World.

But even today's technology has its limits: Israel and Ngozi cannot hear their loved ones responding, of course; this is not a video-phone. And so each side of the family imagines the conversation with the other, as well as the smells and plethora of other particulars that make up not an image but a person, a person one loves from afar. Everyone knows that this kind of love, a fool's love, is the most painful there is. But given the changes wrought by globalization and mass migration, perhaps it is the quintessential love story of our time.

::

After General Sani Abacha's sudden death in 1999, MOSOP and members of the Wiwa clan petitioned the democratically elected government of Osalungen Obasango to claim the remains of Ken Saro-Wiwa, which had been deposited in a mass grave along with his eight MOSOP colleagues after their execution. After considerable wrangling—not the least of which was among opposing factions within MOSOP—Saro-Wiwa's funeral was finally held in April of 2000. Initially, Barine had said that she would be unable to get time off from her three jobs in Chicago to attend the ceremony. Surely, a part of her resisted the stirring up of painful memories—her brother's execution, her husband's death from cancer, the destruction of her homeland. Most immigrants talk of returning home and usually that's all it amounts to—talk. There is the return of fantasy and then the actual thing. Setting foot in the homeland of the present can mean destroying the homeland of the past, of the imagination—for many immigrants the very vision that keeps them focused, paradoxically, on the future. Perhaps for Barine, burying her brother would be like experiencing his death a second time. And then there would be the matter of seeing the barren lots where her restaurants once stood. But when the date for the funeral was finally set, Barine relented. Family and MOSOP members scattered in exile around the world were going, and she was among them.

As recounted in Ken Wiwa's *In the Shadow of a Saint*, Ken Saro-Wiwa's funeral was much more than a family matter. Hundreds came to the airport to receive the Ogoni hero's relatives. Hundreds more paid visits to the Wiwa family's home in the village. And thousands came from all over Ogoniland for the funeral, nearly nine years after Ken Saro-Wiwa was executed. The procession to the cemetery was led by Barine's niece, carrying a cross of hibiscus flowers that she herself picked in the forest. Then came the coffin and Barine's sister, Comfort, carrying a picture of her father. Ken Wiwa writes:

> In the middle of a freshly plowed field was a six-meter concrete tomb lined with white ceramic tiles. As the coffin was lowered into my father's tomb, the ground began to shake and I realized that the crowd was swarming to the edge of the grave . . . there were scuffles and arguments as people fought to get a glimpse of the coffin. When the crowd eventually settled, the archdeacon gave the final orations, but I could barely hear him above the commotion. When he gave me a signal, "Ashes to ashes, dust to dust," I shoveled three small clumps of earth onto the coffin and said a quick, silent prayer.

And so one chapter of Wiwa, and Ogoni history, was finally closed. The MOSOP struggle continues; Shell still wants to exploit oil in the region.

And even if Shell never returned, there are three decades' worth of environmental degradation to deal with, not to mention the rebuilding of Ogoni institutions destroyed by dictatorship, civil war, and colonialism.

For her part, Barine Wiwa-Lawani oversaw the preparations for the elaborate burial feast. In the end, returning home buoyed her mood, as she reconnected with friends and family, soaking up the village intimacy she so sorely lacks in Chicago. But she does not entertain thoughts of remaining in Nigeria. A new path has opened in her life, and she is determined to follow it, even as she swears to never betray her homeland.

"I could not come back and just live in Nigeria," she says. "but I can't just live in America either. I now live between two cultures."

The life of a New American.

::

Israel and Ngozi could not afford to return to Ogoniland for Ken Saro-Wiwa's funeral. While remaining very active in the Ogoni solidarity movement—Israel even travels to Houston, home to Shell's U.S. headquarters, for a MOSOP demonstration—they'd also experienced more than their share of ups and downs in America. Ngozi became pregnant with their third child. Israel trained as a machinist for a factory job, but during a routine physical, the doctor discovered that his blood pressure was dangerously high. During her own visit to the doctor, Ngozi discovered that she is a tuberculosis carrier.

And then comes the moment that every immigrant dreads the most. Israel gets a phone call from home. His older brother, Brendan, has been killed in a car accident. It is a crushing blow. Israel, the eternal optimist, is despondent for months. The only palliative is the presence of his new baby son, Karm. Israel named him after an African tree famous for the strength of its wood.

The Narrative of Exile :: **Ken Saro-Wiwa**

Migrant life places a tremendous strain on family relations. The ceaseless movement over and over the horizon to the next town, the next state, the next country, across rivers and oceans, is stressful enough, as are the long separations between parents and children. Another toll is the disintegration of extended family. The social fabric of Old World societies is made up of the complex network of relations the nuclear family has with the greater family of aunts, uncles, cousins, in-laws. Collective identity based on the geographic proximity of intimate relations – in the village, you may be within walking distance of most of your extended family – starts to crumble as one after another relation takes to the road.

It is one of the terrible ironies of the global era that many migrants undertake their journeys with the goal of providing a better life for their families, yet the separations that result often can work against that very goal. What happens when dad leaves for the States, saying he'll be back in six months, and three years later his presence in the village is only manifest a couple of times a month by a disembodied voice on a long-distance line, or, perhaps, every once in a great while, a VHS videotape greeting?

Parenting is difficult enough when the separated family members live in the same city or country. The challenges multiply when distance between loved ones becomes not just inconvenient, but insurmountable. Father-son relationships have their particular pathos (mythically so, the stuff of literature); add to the classical narrative the unpredictable, unstable, almost incomprehensible set of causes and effects that make up migrant life and you redouble the odds of tragedy.

In the Shadow of a Saint, Ken Wiwa's powerful memoir about growing up the son of Ken Saro-Wiwa, the Nigerian writer and activist executed by the brutal dictatorship of General Abacha in 1995, was lauded by many American reviewers as a "universal" father-son tale. But it is also a very particular narrative shaped by Old World middle-class ambition, by the politics of exile, by – if you like – the very history of colonialism and its present-day incarnation, transnational capital, and the ruin it brings on underdeveloped regions of the world.

Not that the young Wiwa doesn't present us with some familiar father-son tropes. Ken Sr. is the ultimate overachiever; his résumé includes businessman, poet, playwright, novelist, government functionary, and grassroots activist. Wiwa's father's life is his work; at best, Wiwa the son describes him as an aloof figure to his children. He is almost always out of the house on business and when he is home, he's usually in his study, puffing on his pipe as he plots the next business or aesthetic venture.

Contact between father and son is by and large limited to Ken Sr.'s stern lectures about the future. You will attend the best schools, he tells his namesake. You will learn that to get ahead in the world, you need to have a head on your shoulders to counteract the career-debilitating messages of the heart. And, most important, you will place the future of the Ogoni people above all other considerations:

> I never forgot the day he decided to let me in on the meaning of his *and* my life. We were driving around Port Harcourt and he was showing me his business empire. Everything, he revealed, was for one purpose: everything was subservient to his hopes and ambitions for our people. As we drove along the main road in the city, he outlined his vision of the future, and I sank lower and lower in the passenger seat. He was in the driver's seat, his eyes firmly fixed on the road ahead, his horizons expanding as he outlined his vision. When he had mapped out my future, he glanced over and saw me looking grim-faced, my chin buried in my chest . . . I was fourteen years old and I had no idea what he was talking about. . . .

Fourteen years old and already trapped by history and his father's place in it. As "junior" grew into a man, he came to resent his father's rigid imposition of his own historical mantle onto the son. It smacked of a justification of the elder's failures as a father with the most convenient of excuses – politics. Ken Saro-Wiwa was certainly a saint in the eyes of many Ogoni, and in death he became an international symbol of the artist-as-activist who paid the ultimate price for his visionary actions. But in the eyes of his first-born son, the hero had feet of clay, the very model of a man who sets out to save the world but who contradicts that generosity of spirit in his intimate life by betraying his own family.

::

The theme is familiar to me; I experienced a variation of it with my own father. The son of Mexican parents who instilled in him the classic immigrant ethic – work hard, live modestly, hoard your money for the inevitable bad times ahead – my father worked ungodly hours as a lithographer in a print shop. Eighteen-hour days were not uncommon. It was a blue-collar job, but a union job with union wages, and we lived comfortably, better than even my relatively well-off grandparents could ever have imagined. The American dream, in the material sense, was truly ours. But we paid a huge price as a family for that comfort. It wasn't just my father's absence but also how the stress of work influenced his presence at home. Over the course of a decade, his daily habit of two martinis after work to "wind down" turned into an alcoholic binge that led to rehab and a family crisis. I seethed with rage against my father for many years, feeling that despite his Herculean efforts to provide for the family he had failed in something more essential: to support his family emotionally and spiritually. Like Ken Sr. instructing Junior, my father distilled for me his version of the meaning of life, and like Junior, I thought my father was a hypocrite. Junior rebelled, and so did I. It is probably why I am a writer today.

::

When his son was fourteen, Ken Sr. moved the family to England so the children could have an education in the erstwhile empire's best schools. It was in England that Junior began to experience a variation of what DuBois called "double consciousness . . . this sense of always looking at one's self through the eyes of others, of measuring one's soul by the tape of a world that looks on in amused contempt and pity." The immigrant child has only two choices when suddenly faced with his other in the new country: adapt or rebel. Assimilate or resist. The older one is when one emigrates, the less of a choice one has; but the child, who is parachuted into the heart of the new culture via its educational institutions, receives conflicting signals. Two enormous histories collide in public and in private (at school and at home); the child is pulled in opposite directions.

Junior wanted to fit in. I know the feeling. I arrived for my first day of kindergarten lagging behind my classmates in English skills, and from that first bitter day of being singled out as "different," I did everything I could to mimic the foreign culture that had suddenly surrounded me in my new public life. While I confronted the legacy of anti-Mexican sentiment in 1960s California, Junior had the much more painful shock of encountering the thick residue of colonialism in Britain:

This son of a proud African sat in agonized silence through the film *Zulu* as my friends cheered the men in the heavy, starched stiff uniforms that seemed so inappropriate for the blistering heat of Africa, fighting off wave after wave of swarming, menacing Zulus who never spoke, never had any character or humanity. . . . As I watched in the darkened silence of a room in northern England, Africa tugged at me, reminding me that no matter how much I wanted to be like my friends, I was more like those Zulu warriors. I hated the film – I wanted to denounce it there and then

– but I kept my mouth shut while my friends probably absorbed the message that they were God's chosen race.

The irony is that even the immigrant child who chooses to "fit in" is still a rebel – against the maternal culture and its guardians (in Junior's case, of course, represented by his father):

... Since my father had placed himself and Africa between my determination to be one of "us" [with his English classmates], it was probably inevitable that Africa and my father would become one and the same thing in my mind. When I chose to reject my African identity, I was only rebelling against my father.

The argument between father and son begins in Junior's adolescence and continues until Ken Sr.'s execution, and that is why we have *In the Shadow of a Saint*: denied a resolution of the argument while his father was alive, Junior continues the discussion after his death. The book often reads like the transcription of a dialogue that has transcended death itself.

During Junior's college years in England, Ken Sr. reaches the apogee of his political activism. He helps to found MOSOP, the most important political movement in the history of the Ogoni, which is christened with a multitudinous rally that Ken Sr. addresses with stirring oratory. The rally, held on January 4, 1993, was the birth of the movement, and it set in motion a rapid series of events that would end with Ken Sr.'s execution barely two years later.

The story behind the death sentence carried out on Ken Saro-Wiwa is as complex as Nigerian history itself, but in the end it comes down to the wills of two men: dictator General Abacha and Saro-Wiwa himself. Abacha assumed power in late 1993 and sought to prove to multinationals like Shell – with whom the Nigerian ruling class had divided the spoils of its oil-rich Delta region for decades – that the country, after a period of instability, was suitable once again for foreign investment. Political actors like Ken Saro-Wiwa stood in the way. It is not hard to guess the outcome of a battle between a dictator with a huge security apparatus at his disposal and a quixotic "minority" writer (in a land dominated by Igbo, Yoruba, and Muslims, Ogonis are marginal in numbers as well as political and economic power, notwithstanding the rich oil deposits on Ogoni land). In Third World dictatorships, the sword can easily smite the pen – almost always with the abetting, if not the masterminding, of a First World power.

With the movement in Ogoniland blossoming, Ken Sr. urges Junior to return home immediately after finishing college to stand at his father's side in the Ogoni struggle. Things were getting serious in Nigeria. Ken Sr. was detained on two occasions by Abacha's goons and interrogated unto physical and emotional collapse. Increasingly, it seemed that Abacha was determined to dispatch with the Ogoni movement altogether. Armed government forces began firing upon demonstrators trying to keep Shell Oil from resuming operations in Ogoniland. The death toll rose into the hundreds.

But Junior resists his father's call to arms. For the son, the personal has become too political, and vice versa. Upon graduation, he tells his father that he is thinking of enrolling in journalism school. In fact, Junior has become more apolitical in direct proportion to his father's increasing involvement in the Ogoni cause back home. And it is obvious in the battle of wills and wits between father and son that Ken Sr. has done a terrible job of selling Junior on his ideals. On Christmas Day in 1993, Ken Sr., in London at the time, declines an invitation to a dinner hosted by Junior and his live-in partner, Olivia Burnett, declaring that a fast would be more appropriate given the circumstances in the homeland. However father intends the message, the son takes it as a violent personal – not political – rejection.

The last time Junior saw his father was in early 1994. Junior returned to Nigeria to support his brother Gian, who'd had a nervous breakdown and contracted malaria to boot. One day, Ken Sr. was to have accompanied Gian on a visit to the doctor. When Junior asks how the appointment had gone, he is told that his father missed it altogether. The long-simmering rage he'd held for years is on the verge of exploding. Waiting for his father to arrive home, Junior rehearses the brow-beating speech he will give. But when Ken Sr. finally arrives, Junior sees a pitiable imitation standing in for father-tormentor:

> His tie was hanging loosely around his neck, the old brown coat looked shabbier than ever, and he was struggling with a pile of documents. He paused in the doorway when he saw me, smiled nervously, and walked into the sitting room.

And the confrontation Junior rehearsed in his imagination proceeds like this:

> "Have you been to see Gian?" I barked at his back, following him into the lounge. He hauled his briefcase onto the dining table, took off his coat, and glared at me. I stared him down and he backed off. He sat down and started rifling through the papers on the table. He looked broken, almost pitiful, as he absent-mindedly patted the documents strewn on the table. After a few moments, he glanced up at me plaintively. That look is frozen in my mind. It still haunts me, because I suddenly saw through my father. His hair was matted, there were flecks of gray stubble on his chin, and his eyes looked tired and bloodshot. In that moment, I saw my father for what he was: an old man struggling to meet the incredible personal and political demands on him.

It was the last time Junior ever saw his father. The two men never had the opportunity to sit and say what each had to say. But a kind of reconciliation began when Ken Sr. was arrested for the final time, convicted in a sham trial, and sentenced to death. Father and son begin the most intimate dialogue of their lives – in epistolary form. Ken Sr. begins the communication with a missive from prison, a rather impersonal distillation of the events surrounding his conviction. Junior answers perfunctorily. (He says he is trying to keep Ken Sr.'s cause — which has now been taken up by such groups as Amnesty International and PEN International — in the British media; but privately, he frets that he's not doing enough.) The second letter Ken Sr. sends ends with an uncharacteristically personal and wistful note:

> . . . The exhilarating thing is the total support of the Ogoni people and the international community. It makes my suffering worthwhile. I doubt that's much comfort to young children who need the attention and care of their father or wives who require the same. But then, to everyone his fate. How I wish we could choose our parents! Keep smiling. God bless you.

To which Junior responds with . . . silence. The son's ego does a tremendous job at keeping the tangled emotions for his father at bay. But, of course, Junior can never completely rid himself of the man who continues to disrupt Junior's escape from fate often in the most unexpected moments. Such as when he proposes to Olivia Burnett on October 10, 1994. After accepting the proposal, Olivia knowingly asks what the date is. Junior shrugs. "It's October 10," she tells him. "It's your father's birthday."

Soon afterward, Ken Sr. writes again from prison, a letter containing all of twelve words:

> Dear Junior, I have not heard from you in months. Your father.

"In that anguished letter," writes Ken Wiwa, "I felt his pain, his anger. He must of thought that I abandoned him. I threw it in the bin. I felt my anger was justified, but the letter sat in the bin, insisting that I stand up for my father."

Indeed, that minimal missive was the turning point in the relationship between father and son. History helped. Ken Sr. languished in prison for months, without recourse to legal representation or even the doctor's care his deteriorating health demanded. Appeals from human-rights advocates fell on the deaf ears of a demented dictator. That the regime could actually carry out the death sentence began to seem a real possibility. Something in both men broke. Once again, it was Ken Sr. who made the first entreaty, penning a long prison letter that belongs in the anguished canon alongside the epistles written from incarceration by Oscar Wilde or Wiwa's compatriot and Nobel Laureate Wole Soyinka.

> Dear Son,
> This is going to be a longish letter . . . written in a hurry because I live by the minute, unsure what my captors will do next. The intention is to destroy me. I am presently in what should be called a "hothouse," a filthy, rat- and cockroach-infested longish room where I'm held in solitary confinement. The last time I was here was in the early days of my arrest. [Back then] I was in chains. . . .

He goes on to write of "divine intervention" in the form of prison guards who smuggle him bedding and books (one is *Papillon*). And then words that surely dug deeply into Junior's soul:

> I don't know if I've succeeded in giving you a sense of the barbaric system sitting on top of a people, dehumanizing them, turning them to the lowest of beasts. . . . In spite of the struggles of the few, this situation will persist for the next hundred years if all the people have not been ground to dust by then. Terrible vision, isn't it? My joy (and yet it is not such joy, come to face it) is that I gave you, my children, a choice to escape this horror. But then can you be happy in the West? Are the adulation and respect I enjoy here not preferable to the discrimination and dim prospects the West offers you, in spite of all your education? I don't know,

dear son, but I would have wished that Ogoni (if nowhere else), small, extremely rich, and with an industrious and humorous population, could be allowed to develop at its own pace, using its resources, human and material, for its progress. It would be a wonderful home to all its people. . . .

The emotional impasse finally broken, Junior responds with a letter finally venting his feelings about the pain his father caused his mother with workaholism and philandering. He also found the courage to write him that he was marrying Olivia — which he did with trepidation, fearing a nationalist (and racist) response from his father (Olivia is white). On Christmas Eve of 1994, Ken Sr. penned his response, in which he accepts responsibility for his failures as father and husband. He also reverts to his usual hectoring tone and tells his son, basically, to get a life (". . . you were not hard-working enough, failed to save money and were generally idle"). His final words clearly intimate that he senses destiny has taken hold of the reins of his life. "So to the end, you can rest assured that I am in good spirits, quite clear as to what I want and convinced that neither torture nor jail, nor death, can fail my cause."

Junior, who at this point had graduated college and started working at a newspaper, quit his job the next day. For the next year, he became his father's spokesperson, representing his case before any media outlet that listened and even in elite back-channel diplomatic circles. He traveled incessantly for months, gaining audiences with heads of state. It was then that Ken Jr. realized that his father had been right about some things after all. The life of a young man with an emotional pendulum instead of a compass suddenly took on the gravitas of a mature man. And Ken Jr. was doing it in his father's name.

Ultimately, Ken the son represents Ken the father as a complex subject. This man of small stature (he was only five-foot-one) makes up for it with the ego typical of visionaries — indeed, perhaps it is a necessary evil in great people. He verges on the manic, passing from raging to plaintive like a quick fade in a film. As a father and a husband, his flaws are many and obvious: a womanizer, a man who apparently doesn't know the difference between inspiring a child and terrorizing him. Yet despite these faults, his public persona rises to great heights, and ultimately Ken Sr.'s political vision – economic, cultural, and environmental justice, and democracy not just for the Ogoni but for all of Nigeria's far-flung peoples – is the greatest gift that he bequeaths to Junior.

Just a couple of years earlier Junior, alienated in the extreme from Ken Sr., had taken the bold – and a tad melodramatic – step of legally changing his name from Ken Saro-Wiwa Jr. to, simply, Ken Wiwa. When he informed his father – via one of the letters they exchanged when he was incarcerated – the elder was furious. "No one will ever know that you're my son." Which, of course, was also a bit melodramatic, but such is the language of love-hate relationships.

But now, for the first time, it seemed that Ken Jr. knew the answer to the query with which he begins the book: "My father. Where does he end and where do I begin?" He was Ken, son of Ken, for he was both father and son. A part of and apart from his namesake.

The whirlwind tour on behalf of his father ended at the Commonwealth Heads of Government Meeting in November 1995. Luminaries such as Archbishop Desmond Tutu and Wole Soyinka helped Junior lobby leaders for a bold, collective statement of the Commonwealth against the Abacha government's death sentence on Ken Saro-Wiwa. The statement never came. The diplomats felt that "constructive engagement" was the more practical strategy.

It backfired. On the morning of November 10, Ken Saro-Wiwa was led to the gallows. "It took five attempts to hang him," his son reports. "His corpse was dumped in an unmarked grave; acid was poured on his remains and soldiers posted outside the cemetery."

According to witnesses, Ken Saro-Wiwa's final words were: "Lord take my soul, but the struggle continues."

Among the many Ogoni who continue the struggle even today is his son.

3 :: Dominican Republic to Great Falls ::
Ricardo Rodríguez and José García

José García

::

MANY YEARS AGO I LIVED IN GUATEMALA CITY, WHICH IS DIVIDED INTO numbered districts. I rented an apartment in la zona 2, which is famous for two things: *el mapa de relieve*, a fantastically detailed topographical map of the entire country that takes up the space of a city block, and *el hipódromo*, the baseball stadium. A lifelong fan, I chose the neighborhood because I wanted to live near the ballpark. I was so close, in fact, that foul balls occasionally landed on the roof. I vowed to attend every game I could while I lived there, and yet like people who move to the beach and never walk along the shore, I rarely sat in the stands.

Of the few games I did attend, one is committed to digital-quality memory: a Pan American Games exhibition tournament between the United States and Cuban national teams. While there was nary a mention of the game in American media, in Guatemala the match took on mythic proportions. The year was 1989, and the United States had just invaded Panama to capture Noriega. For anti-interventionist-minded Latin Americans, this outrage poured salt on the wound of the invasion of Grenada just a few years earlier, not to mention an entire century of Monroe Doctrine militarism. The Berlin Wall had not yet fallen, and civil wars raged throughout the region, pitting Marxist-trained rebel-peasants against Reagan-backed "freedom-fighting" peasants. To up the ideological ante of the moment, the Cuban Revolution had just undergone one of its most serious crises—the trial (and ultimate execution) of Colonel Arnaldo Ochoa, a decorated military hero turned drug runner (or so Castro said).

And so as the players of the Cuban and American teams took to the field surrounded by an overflow crowd so huge that the base runners could scarcely avoid crunching fans' toes with their cleats, you knew that this was no mere sporting event. Some serious historical scores were going to be settled in *el hipódromo* that afternoon.

If you've never been to a baseball game in Latin America, toss any images you may have of going to a ballpark in the States. There are no dugout boxes or stadium clubs with complimentary champagne; all seating is first-come, first-serve. There is no organist piping a tepid rendition of "The Girl from Ipanema," either: Each team hires a crack tropical music crew that stands atop the dugouts and plays at top volume. The bands—separated by only a few yards—do not perform consecutively but rather simultaneously. If one team scores a run, its band plays a celebratory tune, to which the rival band must respond with another number so as to salve the wound and inspire its team and fans to recover from the setback.

The only ones cheering the gringos that day were the musicians of its hired band. On the surface, at least, this was a curious situation. After all, there were Latin American–born players hustling alongside blond, blue-eyed boys on the American team. And everyone sitting on the splintered wood benches in the stands had a close relative or at least knew someone living and working in the States. Indeed, practically everyone in the stands indulged in some aspect of Americana—films, music, TV shows, hamburgers and fries, Coca-Cola, Chevrolets, Levi's. But there's nothing like a little cultural imperialism to fan the flames of nationalism. It was as if the fans sensed that only here and now, on their baseball diamond, did they have a chance to show the States what Latin America was really made of. It was an opportunity for the perennial underdog to become top gun.

The Americans scored first with two runs in the third, causing the fans to practically rend their garments. But the Cubans' all-star team came back and tied the game in the fifth. The score remained that way for the next three innings, provoking white-knuckling tension in the stands. The seesaw turned back toward America in the top of the ninth with a towering solo home-run hit by a towheaded kid who looked like he'd grown up on a farm in Nebraska. The bands played raucously during the mid-inning break in anticipation of the finale.

In the bottom of the ninth, the States sent their ace reliever to the mound, a Paul Bunyan specimen squirting 100-mph watermelon seeds that smacked the catcher's mitt like thunder. He disposed of the first two batters with swinging strikeouts. Still, the home-team band kept rallying the troops, playing a merengue at punk speed. Miraculously, the next Latin American hitter was able to draw a walk.

And then the heavens opened up. Literally. Not a soul moved from their seats in the downpour, despite the very real risk of death by lightning strike. Within half an hour, the clouds lifted, but it only takes that long for a tropical thunderstorm to dump a couple of inches of rain. The players and coaches trotted out to examine the field. The pitcher's mound was flattened, the batter's box a shimmering lake, the outfield a swamp. But it was the infield that caused the most concern. Even the hardest hit grounder would merely sink in the goo. The musicians knocked water out of their horns, and the fans started chanting for the game to resume. The coaches and umpires huddled with the grounds crew, a trio of wizened peasants in whose hands the fate of the game now rested.

In the American majors, there are things like tarpaulins and water scoopers and retractable stadium roofs. In the Old World, there's kerosene. A pickup truck arrived with barrels of it, and in short order, gallons were poured over the infield dirt. It was left to one of the groundskeepers to light the match, drop it, and run for his life.

The infield of *el hipódromo* burst into yellow flames fifteen feet high and coils of black smoke rose over the stadium. For a few moments, the awesome sight stunned everyone in the park, even the band members, into silence. We could feel the heat on our faces, which all glowed from the inferno. And then one of the bands started up again. On cue, the fans began chanting, dancing, utterly delirious, whooping it up before the unlikeliest of bonfire-offerings to the gods of baseball and anti-imperialism: the Burning Infield.

A few minutes later, the dirt was dry as a bone.

When the game resumed, the next Latin American batter hit the first pitch over the right-field wall and won the game.

::

The Cubans' victory over the gringos that afternoon was marvelously ironic. In the century-and-a-half-long season of economic, military, and political competition in the Americas, the U.S. has never lost a game. With relatively little effort—a military intervention here, a monopolized market there—the Americans came to own the better part of Latin America, lock, stock, and barrel. So on the baseball diamond in Guatemala City, revenge was sugar-cane sweet, with the colonial subjects beating the metropole at its own game. Beyond the diamond, the age-old power relationship remains unchanged. There is "democracy" in places like the Dominican Republic only to the extent it is convenient for the U.S.; there remains abject poverty across the continent precisely because a significant redistribution of wealth is not part of the American democratic game. Latin America must play by our rules, on the diamond and off. The current omnipresence of Latin American players in the major leagues speaks volumes about how, even in the realm of desire, it's the Americans who call the shots: those heroic foreigners are still playing "our" game, after all.

You could even say that Latin American major leaguers, for all their celebrity, are filling much the same role as Latin American migrant farmworkers: doing a job that Americans increasingly won't. Though in this case, it's a job that fills a hole in our psyche—our pop mythology— and not just our industry. In the U.S., baseball was once the place where the pot-bellied and the lanky achieved athletic grace. Today, the typical player's physique is more like the Incredible Hulk. Sport in the U.S. has become utterly fixated on the body as an end unto itself—training gurus; Byzantine gym rituals; diets that count each and every gram of fat, sugar, and fiber; steroids and countless other substances legal and contraband help to flatten, tone, "shred," and make of the body's natural form a foreign object—rather than a subject with a narrative onto which fans inscribe their own longings, which is how myths are made. How can a fat or gawky kid today relate to the cyborgs on the field of their dreams? What made baseball great in America was precisely that its grandeur seemed within reach of everyone. In every neighborhood there was a Ruth or DiMaggio waiting for his shot at glory.

Much has been said of baseball's fading star as the American national pastime, and I think the manipulation of the body is part of its fall. But in other parts of the world, the magical combination of bat, ball, glove, and kid can still create myth.

Take Ricardo Rodríguez and José García, two top Dodgers prospects in the Dominican Republic. They are in many ways today what ballplayers in America once were: working-class kids with not only their own dreams and desires but also those of their families, their neighborhoods, their entire country propelling their bodies toward perfection. They did not train in Nautilus-equipped gyms or pop steroids or even take swings in batting cages when they started out because these things simply were not within reach of boys only a generation or two removed from cutting cane in the fields or hauling sacks in a mill, and who grew up in what is still one of the Caribbean's poorest nations. So poor, in fact, that what

Ricardo Rodríguez and his grandmother in the Dominican Republic

passes for a ball among sandlot kids is a bunch of rolled-up socks. A glove is a folded piece of cardboard. A bat is a bamboo stick.

Freeze frame.

We have heard this story before. Maybe from Sammy Sosa in an interview, or any number of his countrymen, going back in time to the days of "Dominican Dandy" Juan Marichal, a San Francisco Giants pitching ace and the first Dominican superhero in the American majors. The story is a cliché; it does not move us anymore. Yes, yes, banana-republic kid grows up in stultifying poverty, comes to America, and makes it big. A cliché like the words "American dream." Garrett Morris, a comedian who was part of the founding crew on *Saturday Night Live*, drew on the Caribbean ballplayer stereotype in a well-known late-1970s sketch. Suiting up with actual New York pro ballplayers, Morris played the role of "Chico Escuela," an up-and-coming star from the islands. Chico didn't know English very well. His gag line was, "Bays-bohl been berry-berry goo' to me!" I was a teenager then, and I laughed along with everybody else—even as I was aware that my mother's and grandparents' voices were thick with elements of Garrett Morris's feigned immigrant accent. The comedy drew upon several cultural and historical signifiers. Garrett Morris was a black American man—and in the black American typology, there is "innate" athletic ability. Garrett Morris was a black American man playing a black Caribbean man—and in the black Caribbean typology, there is the beachcombing simpleton. The "Chico" character was a menial thrust into stardom and riches—a kind of Horatio Alger tale. We laughed at these stereotypes and, perhaps as Americans, we laughed at ourselves. It was hard to believe that Chico could ever truly be an "American" in the narrow sense—and yet within Chico there were the ghosts of American immigrant history. Our laughter was both a claim on the American exception—we imagine ourselves high on the global stage above the backwardness of the Old World—and an admission that we are actually embarrassed by our origins and whatever of these still lurk inside us.

The more that we as Americans deny history, the more we betray that we are not innocent of it.

::

Few Caribbean peoples could claim innocence from history—American history in particular. The story of how baseball arrived in the Dominican Republic is a matter of migrants, money, and guns.

When Columbus anchored before the island he named Hispaniola, the indigenous Taino royalty that greeted him literally glittered with gold in the form of jewelry. Disease and exploitation decimated the native population within a few short years, necessitating the importation of African slaves. During the early colonial era, Hispaniola was caught in a tug of war between Spain and France—with the English and the Dutch conspiring for their share as well. In the end the island was partitioned, the painful birth of what would become the modern republics of Haiti and the Dominican Republic. Precious metals were exhausted early on, and the island economy underwent a series of transformations from sugarcane and other cash crops to primitive industry and back to sugarcane again at the end of the nineteenth century. The labor intensity of cutting and milling cane created a magnet for laborers from neighboring islands such as Tortola, Nevis, St. Martin, St. Kitt's, and Montserrat. These were islands of the British West Indies, populated by the descendants of slaves whose culture was a blend of the empire's and their own African roots. They were Anglophone and their arrival in the Dominican Republic inspired the typical native response to the foreign other (which is usually at its nastiest when jobs and wages are at stake). Because many were from Tortola, a difficult name for the Spanish-speaking Dominicans to pronounce, they were nicknamed *cocolos*—with the connotation of unwanted foreigner. (Eventually, the *cocolos* took back the epithet and pronounced it with pride.) Among the British cultural artifacts the *cocolos* brought with them were the cricket bat and ball.

Conditions on the cane fields and in the sugar mills, where the *cocolos* dominated, were Dickensian at the turn of the century with the exception of the *tiempo muerto*—the six-month dry season when work was scarce. The season was bad for the labor economy, but good for sports: The *cocolos* organized cricket teams, and the game soon caught on among the Dominican mulatto (Spanish-African) majority. Long before the Americans arrived with baseball, the *cocolos* had sown its seeds in the sugar plantations.

"It's sugar that makes [Dominican] baseball so sweet," Rafael Avila, the domineering head coach of the Los Angeles Dodgers' Las Palmas training camp, tells historian Rob Ruck in *The Tropic of Baseball: Baseball in the Dominican Republic*. "Just like in Cuba, but more so."

The Dominican economy at the turn of the century floundered after decades of foreign exploitation and avaricious native regimes. By the early 1900s, the island had accrued a massive foreign debt, and the custom of merely issuing more paper money only exacerbated the situation. The United States, seeking to expand its influence in the Antilles (and drive the vestiges of European colonial interests out for good), saw the Dominican Republic's vulnerability and made its move, essentially tethering its economy to Washington. In 1916, when political instability on the island threatened the arrangement, the Marines arrived and set up camp for the next eight years. At the end of the intervention, about 80 percent of the sugar industry was firmly in American hands, as were the reins of political power—as they would be for the better part of the twentieth century.

The neocolonial relationship with the United States transformed the Dominican landscape. Subsistence farming was marginalized by cash crops, sending countless peasants to try their luck in the cities; those who remained unemployed had no choice but to cross the Caribbean and try their luck in the States. During the rule of dictator Rafael Trujillo (1930–1961), the Dominican Republic actually bought back much of the Americans' holdings on the island, but these wound up in a vast monopoly that Trujillo himself owned and promoted with protectionism on the one hand and vicious political repression on the other. When sugar prices plummeted in the mid-1950s, opposition to the regime intensified, fanning fears in the U.S. of a Communist takeover. After Trujillo's assassination, relatively free elections brought Juan Bosch, a progressive, to power, but he was in office only seven months before he was deposed by a military coup d'état. When Bosch's supporters tried to reinstate him in 1965, the U.S. invaded in the name of big capital, and Dominican democracy became yet another Cold War casualty. In a unique twist, the United States actually allowed for significant numbers of Dominicans to emigrate, reasoning that a safety valve for "Communist" agitation was necessary. The vast majority of this first wave of emigrants (subsequent waves would come during the pro-business Balaguer regime of the sixties and seventies and the economic crisis that accompanied the more progressive Gúzman regime in the early eighties) found its home in New York, a baseball town if there ever was one.

As long as Ricardo and José continue moving up the professional baseball ladder, they will never have to live in a sprawling, working-class district like Washington Heights, the uptown Manhattan home to the largest Dominican population abroad. It is a vibrant neighborhood, truly a "little Santo Domingo," but it is also the poorest such enclave in New York. According to a study by Columbia University, the median income of the Dominican population is the lowest among all racial and ethnic groups in the city. In the late 1990s, unemployment hovered at 19 percent, and 45 percent of Dominicans lived below the poverty line—more than double the city's average, according to the study.

In the end, Washington Heights is very much an American phenomenon, born of decades of almost total U.S. political and economic domination over the island—and over the immigrant enclaves on American soil. At home and abroad, Dominicans have had no choice but to play our game.

::

The Dominican Republic's complex colonial history is reflected in the modern nation's syncretic identity. There are light-skinned descendants of criollos, mulattoes, black Africans, and even the remnants of what was once a significant population of Sephardic Jews. Mulattoes are by and large Catholic because of the Spanish influence, but many *cocolos*, who had once been subjects of the British Empire, profess the Protestant faith. The Spanish language dominates, but the *cocolo* influence sprinkled English throughout the island as well. So did the U.S. company bosses, technicians, and, of course, the Marines—who, as it happens, also brought a love of baseball, which eventually replaced the *cocolo*'s cricket as the national sport. The island's proximity to Cuba (whose own passion for baseball predated the Dominicans') also promoted the game, and the example of the American Negro League, which regularly toured the Caribbean islands in the early twentieth century, inspired Dominican mulattoes and blacks with the example of great African American athletes.

According to author Rob Ruck, nearly one-tenth of today's major leaguers hail from the Dominican Republic, making this country of eight million by far the largest foreign exporter of baseball talent. More than half a century after Jackie Robinson broke the color line in Brooklyn, another line has been crossed: Today, there are more Dominicans in American baseball than African Americans. And the Dominican Republic will continue to dominate: Some 36 percent of players in the minor leagues were born and raised and tossed their first ball on the island.

Ricardo Rodríguez and José García live in Campo Las Palmas, the Los Angeles Dodgers' training camp in the Dominican Republic. The Dodgers were the first major-league team to open a facility here in 1976; most teams have since followed suit. Both eighteen, Rodríguez (a handsome kid with a ninety-two-mile-an-hour fastball) and García (an outfielder with a golden arm and the potential for Sammy Sosa–like power hitting) were each signed for a modest bonus of $5,000, and they earn about $1,000 a month at camp —far less than would be paid prospects of

Ricardo with former L.A. Dodgers manager Tommy Lasorda

similar talent in the United States. (Nevertheless, from the Dominican point of view even these paltry numbers represent definite upward mobility in a country whose average per-capita income is $1,600 *a year.*) This is one reason why the Dodgers came to the island in the first place—they save millions of dollars by training talent for cheap in the Third World. (American prospects often secure six-figure bonuses.) When businesses stress the bottom line too much, however, ethical lines are often crossed, and the Dodgers are no exception. In the last five years, the MLB commissioner's office investigated the team at least three times for signing underage players. A prospect can only be signed after his sixteenth birthday. One Venezuelan prospect was allegedly signed when he was just fourteen and, according to a ruling by the commissioner's office, the team knowingly recruited star infielder Adrian Beltré, from the Dominican Republic, when he was fifteen.

Las Palmas is run much like a military camp. Players bunk in a dormitory and are marshaled across the field by coaches turned drill instructors. Rafael Avila, the major leagues' first Latin American–born scout (he hails from Cuba), a gruff, big-jowled man, is the George Patton of Las Palmas. He emphasizes that the training is as much cultural as it is athletic.

"In the past, when the players traveled from Dominican Republic to the U.S., 99 percent of them failed," he says in the "mess hall" as players quietly chow down in his presence. "They fail because of poor work habits, language problems, and poor table manners. We need to teach them how to hold silverware properly. Not to hold the fork as if it were a shovel to shove sand with. We teach them not to lower the mouth to the fork like an animal."

Avila notices a prospect wearing a trendy Tommy H.–like skullcap. "What's that he's wearing?" he asks one of his lieutenants. The underling explains that the player, who is black, wears it to cover kinky hair straightened by Vaseline. "You send him home tomorrow," Avila orders. "I've told him several times not to bring it. He's suspended."

There is something terribly troubling about the "cultural" training at Las Palmas. A racial divide—with the clear implication of which race is privileged—permeates the atmosphere. The coaches are mostly white Americans, or, in the case of Avila, criollo Latin Americans. The prospects, of course, are mulatto and black. While the camp's facilities are state of the art, in the Caribbean context, the dormitory eerily recalls plantation living quarters or, worse, the galley of a ship.

The players are told in no uncertain terms what their place is. When Ray Rapenda, the jocular and likeable Las Palmas English teacher, holds a workshop on gender etiquette in America, he invites Denise, an attractive white American woman who works on the island as a Peace Corps volunteer, to talk to the prospects. When she enters the classroom, Ray walks up to her and tries to plant a kiss on her cheek. She mock-slaps him, but the contact is loud enough to be heard by the students, who laugh hard.

"What are you doing?" Denise exclaims, while Ray's face registers theatrical surprise. "What are you doing kissing me? Since when do you kiss white people in the States?"

The skit done, Denise speaks directly to the players, explaining that it's just not the American way for a man to kiss a woman he's just met. The players settle down, soberly taking this information in. Doubtlessly, Ray and Denise think that they're looking out for the players' best interests. After all, there is indeed a difference in etiquette between the Old World and the New. But the skit is also unmistakably "racialized." Ray is white, but the players he's representing in the skit are mulatto and black. The implication is obvious—and dances around the edges of the centuries-old racialized psycho-sexual dynamic between black and white.

Not that Ricardo and José are dwelling on these issues at the moment. They are eighteen years old, after all. They dream about baseball, America, and girls, not necessarily in that order. They have been whisked out of their homes (García is from a tough barrio in Santo Domingo, and Rodríguez from a humble rural background) and are a step away from standing on the field of their dreams in America—and earning seven-figure salaries.

"Poor people's dreams are profound things," says José, who is the same age as Ricardo but looks and acts younger. Profound because he knows that there is only one shot at pulling himself and his family out of poverty for good: He must prove to his instructors at Las Palmas that he has the right stuff within three years. If he does not graduate to playing in the minors in America by then, team policy dictates that he must be released. Dodger scout Rafael González found García by doing what he does best—literally beating the bushes throughout the island. Sometimes, in remote rural areas, he'll ride horseback through cane fields to check out a prospect. When he saw José, there was no doubt in his mind that he had the raw materials to make it. But José's progress at Las Palmas has been halting at best. An outfielder with an excellent arm (Rafael Avila compares it with Raúl Mondesí's, a former Dodger star who came up through Las Palmas), the brass is counting on him to deliver power hitting. But according to his coaches, who scribble copious notes on virtually his every move, José has not come through.

The pressure José is under may have something to do with it. He is told again and again how everyone is counting on him to succeed. He hears it from his mother, Lala, a loving woman who nevertheless openly expresses her doubts about his prospects in José's presence. And he hears it, perhaps most of all, from Rafael Avila.

"Don't think that just because you're getting a salary for the first time that you've made it in the major leagues," he tells the players in one of his frequent "inspirational" talks. "There are thirty-five players [in the majors] that came from this camp. Pedro Martínez earns seventy-seven million dollars; Raúl Mondesí, sixty million. And the list goes on. This is a test; if you fail here, you will return to your villages broken. Your family's future is in your hands."

After much debate about José's chances, the coaches decide that maybe he's not cut out to be a power hitter after all. They announce that he will be retrained as a pitcher. "This is what I feared the most," says a frowning Lala when José visits home to tell her the news. But she relents when she notices the crestfallen look on her son's face. *"Negrazo,"* she coos to him, using the black-Caribbean term of endearment, as she strokes his close-shaved head. After José shuffles out into the streets of the barrio, Lala talks of how many kids she's seen wind up with their baseball dreams broken. "When the kids are about fifteen years old, if they're strongly built, the scouts start telling them that they can be baseball players, that they can make a lot of money like Sammy Sosa, like Pedro Martínez. So they think they can make money faster playing, doing anything except going to school. Most of them wind up as nobodies. Vagabonds. And people say about them, 'He used to be a good ballplayer. . . .'

"His success will be our success," Lala adds, echoing Rafael Avila. "His failure will be our failure."

The Dominican Republic may produce more ballplayers per capita than any other nation (including the United States), but it is an obvious truth that the vast majority of kids that dream hardball dreams will never make it out of the country, much less graduate to the major leagues. And once that dream is denied to young adults like José García, there is really nowhere else to turn. The Dominican economy, like that of most Caribbean nations, survives by and large on the tourism industry—and on money sent back home by Dominicans working in the States, not in baseball but in the service industry.

On the streets of the barrio, José passes by crews of kids and elders playing checkers and dominoes. The beat of a merengue number softly wafts out of someone's house. José moves his feet modestly to the rhythm, dancing by himself on the street corner.

::

When the training coach walks into the clubhouse with a sheet of paper in his hands announcing that he has some "surprises," every player knows immediately what they are. "I have here in my hand a provisional list—*pro-vi-sion-al*—of players who are going to the States . . ."

Ricardo Rodríguez is among the six names on the list. Ricardo rushes back home to tell his mother María the good news. "I'm going!" he says. "You're going!" she echoes, and hugs him ecstatically. He's got only a few days to take care of personal business before his scheduled departure. He pays a visit to the barber shop, and then calls on his girlfriend. (Earlier, he'd told us that he'd once had four girlfriends, but that things were too complicated that way.) "I'm going," he tells her. "You're going," she responds, proud and heartbroken at the same time. And then the most difficult visit of all—to his grandmother's house, where he spent much of his childhood. It seems as if the old woman, who now lives alone, senses that she may never see Ricardo again. It's moments like these that underscore the distance between America and much of the rest of the world: from his grandmother's point of view, it seems as if Ricardo is embarking upon a journey that will take him to an impossibly distant land, like a Spanish explorer. Ricardo's sense of time and space is altogether different, of course—he feels like he could skip a stone across the Caribbean Sea to Florida—but he's also never been on a jet plane.

Ricardo dresses in a new suit for the flight. Players are expected to be well-groomed (Rafael Avila, no doubt, has drilled this into their heads), but Ricardo dresses up also in honor of the occasion of his departure. Even for those migrants in the world today who have the luxury of flying to their new homes (and flying back to their hometowns for visits), the custom of wearing one's best for an important journey still holds. Frequent-flying business types only go formal if they absolutely must; most Americans jump on a plane as casual as can be. The migrants are bringing a touch of the Old World to the new, dressing as for a family portrait. It is a moment to be savored, remembered in later years. I recall my grandfather once taking me to an octogenarian tailor in El Salvador to be fitted for a new suit before returning to the States after a particularly long sojourn in the Old Country. I arrived in the U.S. looking like I'd stepped out of a time machine. I only wore that suit once. But I remember everything about the day that I wore it.

Now at the airport in Santo Domingo, at the boarding gate after completing his good-byes, Ricardo stands alone at a window looking out upon the rain-slicked tarmac. His temperament is almost always upbeat and relaxed, but now he is wordlessly pensive. When the jet engines go full-throttle, he instinctively crosses himself.

José and teammate on the road

"*Allende el mar . . .*" the Spanish explorers used to say, Across the sea
. . . is the future.

::

Fast forward to . . . Great Falls, Montana, a small town north of Helena.
The Los Angeles Dodgers have a single-A minor-league team here. It is
a long way from the Dominican Republic, and José García and Ricardo
Rodríguez are among a handful of Dominicans in this northern outpost
of 60,000. After a stint in the Arizona Instructional League, Great Falls
is the latest stop on Ricardo's seemingly unstoppable journey to the
majors. José, meanwhile, has a new lease on life as a potential Dodger

pitcher. "My heart is in the outfield," he still says, but he has no choice but to use his arm's obvious strength to fulfill the wishes of the Dodgers who, like all major-league teams these days, are facing a dearth of pitching talent.

In the minor leagues, players live with "house-parents," big-hearted fans who provide room and board for a largely symbolic fee from the clubs. (While it is a time-honored tradition with obvious benefits for both players and "parents," it is also yet another way major-league teams save loads of money.) Ricardo and José, barely conversant in English despite Ray Rapenda's best efforts back in Las Palmas, room at the home of Ole and Marie Mackey, a sweet elderly couple with practically no working Spanish.

The presence of Ricardo, José, and their Caribbean cohort in Great Falls might be unusual, but it is no longer a unique migrant experience in the U.S. The 2000 Census provided ample evidence of a dramatic demographic shift. In the course of a decade, immigrants from Latin America, Africa, and Asia spread out from the traditional portals of major cities and into the American heartland. On a cross-country car trip a few years ago, I ran into Punjabis in Arkansas, Salvadorans in Utah, Hmong in Pennsylvania. Social scientists have various theories to explain migrant movement, from neo-Marxist emphasis on the magnetic attraction-repulsion force of the labor economy to models that point to complex, transnational migrant networks where the migrants themselves are the ultimate protagonists. Others suggest that the influence of globalization is relevant also; First-World goods and pop culture that flood developing-world markets may provoke movement by the sheer power of suggestion. In the particular slice of migrant life at hand, it would seem that a bit of each of these is at work—but as we have seen, centuries of colonial intrigue were integral to setting the stage for the Dominicans' American baseball dreams.

But history, for all its grand designs, always gives way to the present and the minutiae of the mundane. For Ricardo, José, and their house-parents, this means a crash-course in intercultural communication. Language is the immediate hurdle, which is relatively easily overcome with pidgin Spanish, pidgin English, and exaggerated pantomime. Food is another problem. The heartland meals served up by the Mackies do not agree with the Dominican palate; soon José and Ricardo attempt to show Marie the finer points of Caribbean-style cooking—as best they can as macho men who've never spent much time in the kitchen.

For all the obvious contrasts between the two cultures, religion offers a bridge. The Mackie's Catholic congregation receives their Latin brethren with open arms, and José and Ricardo even wind up singing in the church choir. All in all, the Dominicans are received with great enthusiasm in Great Falls, a town that can now officially count itself part of the global realm.

Because of their near-hero status, Ricardo, José, and their teammates (as close as Great Falls will get to hosting major-league talent) find themselves in a state of migrant grace: They don't feel the pressure most foreigners do to shed their Old World ways and "act American." Many immigrants learn to hide their maternal culture in public—or are forced to. A colleague of mine, a Mexican musician who holds a day job at a Crate & Barrel outlet in Los Angeles, was recently told by her African American supervisor that she had to "ask permission" before speaking Spanish in front of the well-heeled gringo customers, whose precious yuppie space would presumably become déclassé if the employees uttered the Old World vowels. (California law now prohibits language restrictions in the workplace: The yuppies will have to learn to live with the Old World after all.) The only space for migrants to be fully themselves is in the privacy of their homes or in the cultural safety of the enclave.

But the Dominicans in Great Falls are liked precisely the way they are. So what if the good people of Great Falls objectify them, sexually or otherwise—at least the Dominicans can be themselves. At a reception at Marie and Ollie's house, Ricardo and José serve as deejays and spin some merengue. Soon they have Marie out on the dance floor, showing her the basic tropical steps.

For the local single women in town, the arrival of the tall, very dark, and handsome athletes creates a small furor. Several are regulars in the stands for workouts and games. Surely, the admonitions from Ray Rapenda and Denise are securely lodged in the players' heads. This does not prevent, however, the complaint of a Great Falls woman against Ramón Martínez (not to be confused with the Dominican star pitcher currently in the majors), one of José's close friends on the Dodgers. The woman claimed that at a house party, Martínez tried to force himself upon her at knifepoint. Martínez denied the charge, but he was arrested and spent several months in jail awaiting a trial in which he was ultimately acquitted. (As far as the Dodgers were concerned, the complaint itself was evidence enough to release him from the team.)

One can imagine the talk in Great Falls in the aftermath of accusation. To their credit, many locals, including Ramón Martínez's house-parents, believed the accused at his word. But unfortunately for the Dominicans, the incident reaffirmed age-old stereotypes about Latin macho lust. The irony is that Dominicans' own racial attitudes are radically different than our own. I discovered this in the Mt. Pleasant district of Washington, D.C., where there was a healthy Dominican enclave until recent gentrification drove most of the immigrants out of the neighborhood. I remember asking a young Dominican kid—dressed in hip-hop regalia— what he thought about being black in America. "But I'm not black!" he protested. "I'm Dominican." A black Dominican rapper saying he wasn't black. Partly, this seemed to be a result of colonial history and the caste-like situation of distrust on the island between light- and darker-skinned blacks. Mulattoes like the young rapper I spoke to claim a separate identity. And yet most people in the U.S. regard the Dominican mulattoes as black, except for African Americans, who by and large consider them Latin Americans. The in-between space the Dominicans occupy may be premonitory for race relations, and the future of the very idea of race, in the United States. The increase in mixed-race marriage (and children), the fact that so many immigrant "people of color" are ambivalent about the American notion of race to begin with, and the demographic changes that mean America is no longer simply a black and white country are signs of what could become in the near future a fundamental shift in the way we see ourselves.

But older notions of race still hold their power. When Ricardo Rodríguez first heard news about the allegations against his teammate, he said his first reaction was "to want to go back home."

For his part, José was clearly shaken by the experience and harbored not a little resentment toward the Dodger higher-ups for their re-action. "If it had been a white player," he says, "things would have been different."

Perhaps. But the main fallout from the incident was that suddenly the Dominicans didn't feel so comfortable in Montana after all. They were, for the first time perhaps, truly aware of the shade of their skin, the accent with which they spoke English, and the idea that maybe kissing a white girl on the cheek could result in a slap (or worse), not in a silly skit but in real life.

::

As of this writing, Ricardo Rodríguez has found a home in the American majors. He was traded out of the Dodgers' minor-league system to the

Cleveland Indians, and saw some action on the field in 2002 and early 2003 before being traded again, to the Texas Rangers, who currently pay him $302,400 a year. It's a far cry from Sammy Sosa's income of $16,875,000, but not bad for a Dominican country kid.

As for José García, he is no longer playing professional baseball. But he did find companionship in America: He married a woman he met in Albany, Georgia during his stint with the local minor league team.

Still, baseball hopes die hard for the Dominicans. It's one of the few American dreams they've been able to, however rarely, achieve.

The Narrative of Exile :: **Juan Luis Guerra**

It is 1988, and I am walking the streets of Mexico City, the midway point between Los Angeles and San Salvador, the twin poles of my political and personal passion. It is summer, the wet season in the great central plateau of Mexico, and I am hanging on a busy corner under a street vendor's plastic tarpaulin bulging with rainwater. I do not remember the exact place, but I'm somewhere along Avenida Insurgentes, the city's main north-south thoroughfare. Surrounding me are dark brown faces, the color of Indian Mexico, the color of a millenary culture and of poverty, of defeat and survival. The vacant stares of elders surviving another day of smog and traffic and asphalt bearing down on the bones of the erstwhile Aztec capital. The toothy smiles of children still innocent of the crushing world into which they've been born.

I am smoking a cigarette through a Mexico City downpour, thinking about the war in El Salvador, which I have been covering as a reporter, and about my Salvadoran lover in Los Angeles, a refugee from that very conflict. I am composing a story in my head about civil war and American interventionism, about having grown up between North and South, East and West, Spanish and English, Capitalism and Communism, the First and Third Worlds. These were the themes that obsessed me, the young writer, at the time. They still do.

Around me, there are a dozen boom boxes, all blasting tunes at distorted decibels, the usual Mexican and tropical romantic classics of the golden era and the pop fluff of the moment. And now a solo sax bends a note that catches my ear, a graceful glissando leading off a midtempo tropical number – not salsa, not merengue or cumbia, but a beat I would later learn was *bachata*, a Dominican pop form that takes its time creating a sensual aura through a curious tension of restraint and abandon. Now comes the lead vocal, a nasally but graceful tenor:

Ojalá que llueva café en el campo
Que caiga un aguacero de yuca y té
Del cielo una jarina de queso blanco
Y al sur una montaña de berro y miel
Oh, oh, oh-oh-oh, ojalá que llueva café

(I wish it would rain coffee in the countryside
That there would come a cloudburst of yucca and tea
From the sky fall a dusting of fine white cheese
And in the south a mountain of watercress and honey
. . . I wish it would rain coffee)

My heart soared with the song. I was transported to Salvadoran plantations become Elysian fields, to worn-down barrios suddenly resplendent with dignity, to a Latin America whose politics matched its honest, sublime cultural legacy. In the lyrics of a three-minute pop song, there were overtones of Neruda's *Residence on Earth* and García-Márquez's Macondo, set to a music recalling the great Latin romantic tradition that is a melding of Spanish, African, and Indian – that is, New World – yearning.

It was my first encounter with Juan Luis Guerra, hands-down the most famous Dominican among Dominicans, on a par with slugger Sammy Sosa and dictator Rafael Trujillo. I thought then, and I write now, that what Dylan did for American pop lyrics, Guerra did, with one song, for Caribbean music – specifically the merengue and bachata beats of the Dominican Republic. *Ojalá que llueva café* was the soundtrack of Latin America that summer, a massive pop hit that defined a moment, like Jefferson Airplane's "White Rabbit" – cautioning about even as it celebrated the Summer of Love – or the unbridled sexuality of Prince's "When Doves Cry" piercing through the neoconservatism of the Summer of Reagan. The year before the Berlin Wall fell, 1988 was a time of utter despair in the southern lands. The Contra war was at its height in

Nicaragua, the civil wars in El Salvador and Guatemala took their terrible tolls, the Mexican peso tumbled, the refugees ("economic" and "political" – a distinction I never understood) amassed at the U.S.-Mexico border. Juan Luis Guerra brought a melodic salve to these wounds, soothed us in ways that no politician or preacher ever could. Everyone heard the song – it blared on street corners and on buses and out the windows of houses, from portable radios accompanying campesinos in the picking fields. Guerra's popularity cut across lines of race and class throughout the Caribbean, Mexico, and Central America: The intellectual grooved alongside the worker. I've never again experienced a pop communion like it.

Latin Americans are de facto exiles: cast out of paradise by the Conquest, denied a unified lineage by the process of *mestizaje*, the physical miscegenation and cultural synthesis brought about by the violent meeting of European, Native American, and African. Guerra seemed to be telling us – through lyric metaphor and the literal mixing of musical styles through which he delivered those lyrics – that perhaps paradise was ours after all, in the very fact of our hybridity:

Somos un agujero
en medio del mar y el cielo
quinientos años después
una raza encendida
negra, blanca y taína
¿pero quién descubrió a quién?

(We're a thin rupture
in between sea and sky
five hundred years later
a glowing tribe
black, white and Indian
but who discovered who?)

The lyrics, by mirroring our desire, assured us it would be requited. The war would soon be over, the smog would eventually lift, the parched fields of the campesinos would grow verdant.

::

El costo de la vida sube otra vez
El peso que baja, ya ni se ve
Y las habichuelas no se pueden comer
Ni una libra de arroz, ni una cuarta de café
A nadie le importa que piensa usted
¿Será porque aquí no hablamos inglés?

(The cost of living goes up again
The peso's down so low it can't be seen
You can't afford to eat beans
Or a pound of rice, or a quarter [pound] of coffee
No one cares what you think
Could it be because we don't speak English here?)

Born in 1957, Juan Luis Guerra was raised in the old middle-class neighborhood of Gazcue in the heart of Santo Domingo, and aside from the occasional North American tour with his band, 4.40, he remains a Dominican denizen. Yet Guerra's lyrics of conscience consistently reflect the very context that has sent hundreds of thousands of his compatriots to Puerto Rico and the U.S. mainland seeking the better life. Dominican hopes that the ouster of long-time dictator Rafael Trujillo in 1961 would usher in an era of expanded horizons for the island's huge underclass diminished with each year that those hopes went unfulfilled, while the numbers of those willing to try their luck in the States increased. Notwithstanding the high percentage of Dominicans who have utilized legal avenues to achieve residency in the U.S., several thousands have also risked the harrowing *balsero* (raft) journey made more famous by Haitian and Cuban refugees, and there are no reliable estimates as to how many become victims of the Carribbean's waters.

According to Census 2000 figures, there are 765,000 Dominicans living in the U.S., with an astounding concentration of some 406,000, or nearly two-thirds the national total, in the New York City region alone. Little Santo Domingo, otherwise known as Washington Heights in uptown Manhattan, is the most visible of the neighborhoods transformed by this immigrant trans-fusion. Ma-and-pa stores are stocked with the yucca and plantains and the salty white cheeses of home; restaurants offer the typical Dominican *fritanga* – fried anything.

And on every street where the Dominicans have achieved critical mass, there is *merengue* and *bachata*, the island's musical patrimony, brought from the island once known as Hispaniola across the Caribbean sea to the isle of Manhattan to blare from the windows of apartment buildings that have hosted immigrants from the world over in the last 150 years. It is testimony to the power of *cultura popular*, as Latin Americans refer to pop culture (placing the emphasis on "popular" in the socio-economic sense, as in *las clases populares*, the working classes) that the experience of migration – American assimila-tionism notwithstanding – does not dissuade the newly arrived from sticking to their "roots."

If anything, the sense of a primordial cultural home is all the more impor-tant outside the context of the homeland, becoming a shield against the alien-ating and often hostile new environment. Out of this form of cultural resist-ance, immigrant enclaves, from Little Italy's to Little Saigon's, have formed throughout American immigration history. In the context of the global, the enclaves appear to be changing from transitory spaces – in the assimilation-ist narrative, way stations en route to the "melting pot" – into more perma-nent, and in some ways, more autonomous zones. Washington Heights, and the Salvadoran enclave of Pico-Union in Los Angeles, and the hundreds of Little Mexicos across America, show no sign of becoming cultural or historical relics whose main purpose is to represent some mythic, essential notion of immigrant-ness to third- generation progeny hungry for "roots" or, more typically, to tourists. Because of complex transnational economic and social connections between the new enclaves and the homeland, immigrants shuttle back and forth with extraordinary frequency, a fact that became poignantly apparent to mainstream America with the crash of American Airlines Flight 587 on November 12, 2001 (some 175 of the 260 people killed were Dominican nationals, most of them residents of the U.S. en route to visit relatives for the winter holidays).

In this scenario, the home away from home is not just a tenuous imitation of the homeland. The second home and the homeland enter into a symbiotic relationship on the economic level – relatives in the Dominican Republic receive over $1.5 billion dollars annually from the U.S., equivalent to 15 percent of the island's GNP – as well as on the cultural plane. The revival of popular forms such as *merengue* and *bachata* occurs precisely because of the diaspora: Young Dominicans in Washington Heights, in cultural terms, can have their cake and eat it too, by melding American pop influences such as techno music, with the music of their parents. Thus, techno-*merengue* arrives on the island when migrants return for a visit. Likewise, tradition is replenished in the American enclaves with the arrival of new migrants bearing the memory of home. The island encompasses not just the national geographic territory, but the existential space between enclave and homeland.

Although Guerra is often celebrated as a nationalist artist – his success almost single-handedly revived Dominican pop after years of deadly commercialized productions – his music is also very much the product of the diaspora. He picked up the guitar as a teenager, serenading the neighborhood in the classic romantic vein. But growing up in the 1960s meant that he was also weaned on American and British pop, especially The Beatles (who, ironically, appropriated Latin rhythms in their early romantic ballads), even though he could scarcely understand the lyrics. He joined the Dominican exodus in the 1970s and arrived in Boston for a stint at the prestigious Berklee School of Music, where he became enamored of jazz forms – an influence that led to his early albums sounding a bit like a Dominican version of Manhattan Transfer.

After completing his studies, he returned to the island. The early 1980s were a transition period in Latin American music. The effervescent protest style (*"nueva canción"*) of the 1960s and 1970s began wearing down into cliché, while puerile imitations of American pop or slick, soul-less salsa predominated in the commercial realm. Guerra's first forays into solo production were largely forgettable. Then, in 1984, Panamanian salsero Rubén Blades, already a veteran of commercial success from his days of working in Willie Colon's band in New York, released *Buscando América*, an album whose impact on the Latin music world was akin to The Beatles' *Sergeant Pepper* or Dylan going electric-guitar at Newport in 1966. Blades's lyrics were full-blown narratives with detailed characterizations, shifting points of view, and an utter connection to the historical moment. One song told of the "disappeared" victims of political persecution, another of an activist priest gunned down by death squads (a thinly veiled allegory about real-life Salvadoran archbishop Oscar Arnulfo Romero, martyred in 1980). By and large, Blades stuck to the standard 6/8 beat of salsa, but accentuated, through a masterful percussion section, the music's African roots; the horn section, on the other hand, developed lines much more melodically complex than the typical tropical band – a nod to American and Latin jazz.

Buscando América was a revelation: Salsa for Blades was not just a danceable form, but a medium for lyric imagination, and a vehicle through which an artist could mirror the social concerns of a people. Juan Luis Guerra clearly took his cue from Blades: Beginning with *Ojalá que llueva café* and on every album since, Guerra wedded his Afro-Caribbean roots with his penchant for American pop and jazz. On the lyrical level, Guerra splits his time between producing finely crafted poems in the romantic tradition –

Quiéreme como te quiero a ti
Dame tu amor sin medida
Búscame como abeja al panal
Y liba la miel de mi vida

(Love me like I love you
Give me your love without measure
Seek me out like a bee does the honeycomb
And savor the honey of my life)

and exploring historical and social themes, such as in this compelling inter-
pretation of a Taíno (Dominican native people) slave chant:

Soy un siervo
No me mates . . .
Fuente de la montaña alta
Ven a nosotros
Fuente de la montaña alta
Mira, ven a ver
Mi corazón
No me mates
Mi corazón
Blanco
Negro
Rojo
Soy un siervo, no me mates

(I'm a servant
Don't kill me . . .
Fountain of the high mountain

Come to us
Fountain of the high mountain
Look, come and see
My heart
White
Black
Red
I'm a servant, don't kill me)

Fifteen years have gone by since Guerra's breakthrough with *Ojalá*; he released several albums through the midnineties, with varying degrees of commercial and critical success (*Bachata Rosa*, released in 1995, was his biggest seller; *Areito*, from 1992, was the most ambitious). Then came a dry spell. Rumors circulated that Guerra had "found God" in the form of an evangelical conversion and renounced popular music. But he reappeared in 1999 with *El Niágara en Bicicleta*, and while the CD jacket is sprinkled with references to *"Jesús, mi Señor y Salvador,"* the music is about as worldly as Guerra has ever been, what with an erotic number that makes extended use of hi-tech metaphors (*Niña, te quiero decir / que en mi PC sólo tengo / un monitor con tus ojos / y un CD-ROM de tu cuerpo . . .* Girl, I want to tell you / that in my PC there's nothing more / than a monitor flashing your eyes / and a CD-ROM of your body), and the title track, a song about one man's experience of the Dantesque Dominican public health system which is, the refrain suggests, like "riding Niagara Falls on a bicycle."

But the one song I'll always remember Guerra for is *Ojalá*. When I think back to the summer of 1988, memory brings harrowing images. In El Salvador, rockets fired from helicopters streaking across the tropical starry night and exploding on a guerrilla encampment in the jungle-thick folds of a volcano. In Mexico City, police clubbing Indian protesters with truncheons. In Los Angeles, freshly arrived refugees sleeping in the basement of a downtown church, their eyes wild with fear and uncertainty and trauma. But Guerra's melody is the sound-track to these scenes, reminding me that in Latin America, we bear the horrors of our trek through the present by carrying a knapsack of memory and hope. In Spanish, *"ojalá"* means, literally, "I hope so." But in Guerra's lexicon, it means more than wishful thinking, passive desire: It is a communal yearning that paves the way toward the future.

4 :: **Mexico to Mecca** ::

The Flores Family

Pedro Flores

::

It is 95 degrees at nine o'clock in the evening in Mecca, California; not unusual for the month of September. Ventura Flores, a woman of forty who looks closer to fifty, sits in the dim light on the front steps of her sister's thirty-foot trailer home, where she, her husband, Pedro, and five of their children, along with her sister and five of her children, live. It is a Friday night, and the kids are glued to the TV inside the stifling-hot trailer. In an effort to save money, the owner of the trailer, Ventura's sister Irma, does not turn on the cooler—not an air conditioner, but a contraption that works by dint of evaporating water, also known as a "swamp cooler." It gets its name from the fact that the evaporative system works wonders when the weather is hot and dry, but if there's even a tad of humidity in the air—such as during the "monsoon" summer months, when towering thunderheads rise over the desert floor—the machine merely redoubles the moisture in the air, creating a "swamp" indoors. The Floreses didn't have any kind of cooler in Mexico, but they also lived not in the desert but in the temperate climes of the central part of the country.

Few people would consider Mecca, a small desert outpost about forty miles southeast of Palm Springs, a paradise. It is some fifteen miles off the interstate; the only reason a tourist would wind up in Mecca is, perhaps, to visit the Salton Sea, a strange body of brackish water created when the Colorado River flooded at the turn of the last century. The river no longer floods, having been manipulated by human hands, dammed and diverted, for hydroelectric purposes—and agribusiness. The fortuitous proximity of Mecca to the California Aqueduct transformed the badlands into a booming agricultural region. That's the reason the immigrants are here. Once a place that attracted only a handful of desert rats, Mecca's population is now overwhelmingly Mexican.

Increasing numbers of immigrants work in such out-of-the-way places—the economy pushes and pulls, from Third World to First, from city to suburb, from coast to interior, from factory to farmland.

There is no movie theater, no mall, only a couple of motels on the outskirts of town. "Downtown," in fact, is not much more than a gas station and a convenience store. Not much for a teenager to do here—and there are plenty of them, hauled in by their migrant parents. Many of them work alongside the elders in the fields well before their eighteenth birthdays. Many of them will not finish high school; if they're lucky, they will attend a couple of night classes to learn basic English. Wound tight with nervous energy—the tension between their desires and the reality of their station in life—some of them turn to the "cholo" lifestyle, emulating the gangsters of East L.A. with oversize pants, bandanas, and badder-than-bad shades. They cruise the dusty streets of town in their dilapidated mobiles looking for action, but they find only the vastness of desert night, an inscrutable black mirror. By day, they take their place alongside everyone else in the fields.

The five working adults of the Flores family (including Ventura's daughters Nora and Lorena, nineteen and eighteen years old, respectively) all work for $6.75 an hour, just a cut above the minimum wage in California, but there are thirteen mouths to feed at home, rent for the trailer park space, and utility bills. The income is barely enough to cover these expenses.

The air is dead without the slightest breeze. The heat radiates up from the ground, from the walls of the trailers, from every solid surface that sat under the white sun all day long. The only sound comes from a couple of TVs and radios, but even these are turned down low. For most of the American workforce, Friday night is time to cut loose, but not for the Mexicans of Mecca. Most of them work six days a week. Saturday is just another workday that will begin well before dawn.

I ask Ventura's daughter Nora, the eldest, what she usually does on a Friday night. "Nada," she says, although she clearly wants to go somewhere, anywhere. When she comes home from a day in the fields, where she crouches alongside her aunt from six-thirty in the morning to about three in the afternoon, she bathes, fixes her hair, and dons makeup, but more often than not she remains in the trailer park, waiting for something or someone that never comes.

The trailer park where the family lives is an unpaved slice of land on the outskirts of town. Because most of the trailers are lit so dimly—low-wattage bulbs mean cheaper electric bills—it is almost impossible to tell that there is a community of about two dozen families here. You can drive past it at night and not notice it, the tiny camp lost in the dusty dark.

It is nearly ten o'clock now, bedtime for the Flores family and for most of Mecca. Since they got off of work, they have bathed, cooked, cleaned, watched TV, and chatted quietly on the steps of the trailer. There is nothing more to do, except sleep, and dream.

::

Mecca was christened either by hopeful pioneers looking to find precious metals in the desert, or by someone with a caustic streak of irony. It is drab and dusty. It's hard to imagine anyone making any kind of spiritual pilgrimage to this Mecca. Of course there are no mosques. There are not even any New Agers who can be found in abundance in the more picturesque landscapes of the California High Desert, about fifty miles north. For most, Mecca is a way station on the rails of their ambition. Many Mexican migrants begin their lives in the States by picking in the fields; the lucky ones "graduate" to service jobs in the city—in restaurants, hotels, construction, and the garment industry. With a lifetime's worth of work, some of these urban workers save enough to buy

Pedro and children in Mecca, California

a house, but not in a middle-class neighborhood. With their wages, they can usually only afford a house in the erstwhile middle-class suburbs of cities like Los Angeles, among the rows of one-story stucco homes where mostly white automobile or aerospace workers once carved out their slice of the American dream. After years of deindustrialization, these peripheral cities south and east of downtown came to be known as the "rust belt." White flight meant lower real-estate values, and the Mexicans arrived.

The Floreses' pilgrimage to Mecca began about thirteen years ago, when Ventura's husband Pedro left his family and hometown in Mexico to make his first trip across the river seeking what Mexicans call *la vida major* (the better life). He roamed the States alone, taking up work in the fields and occasionally in construction. In Spanish, such men are referred to as *solos*, solitary ones. In many ways, they resemble the pioneers or Depression-era wayfarers of lore, but they are not regarded as such by most Americans. Theirs is a Kerouacean tale, many of them logging more miles than Sal Paradise and Dean Moriarty did in *On the Road*, and yet their travels are not mythologized in American literature, with the exception of a handful of Southwest Mexican-American works. By and large, the Mexicans' journeys go unnoticed. But if you were to board a late-night Greyhound bus traversing the rural counties of North Carolina or the Cascade mountains, barreling across the oil fields of Texas or the humid plains of the Mississippi River valley, you'd probably wind up sitting next to a quiet, young, brown-skinned man with almond-shaped eyes dressed humbly in T-shirt, jeans, and old sneakers, carrying his belongings in a small vinyl pack. His English would be halting, but he'd smile at everything you say. And if you understood Spanish well enough, he'd probably tell you that he just finished a watermelon harvest in Kentucky and is now moving on to the citrus orchards of Florida. Or that he's heading home to his *pueblo* after eight months' work in the strawberry fields of northern California, to see his son, who was born while he was on the road. Or that he got tired of working in a restaurant in L.A. for less-than-minimum wage and is striking out for the Midwest to check out reports from fellow migrants that there are higher wages to be had in meat-packing. Or in a chicken ranch . . . or at a lawn-grass farm. The country is vast and its economy as diverse as its landscape and people. To find a job all one has to do is take to the road, and Pedro Flores took to it.

He didn't want to travel alone. Mexicans never quite had the equivalent of the American tradition of macho adventurers or hobos. The Mexican migrant journey, like most all Old World journeys of necessity, is not an end unto itself, but rather a means to lift the family out of poverty in the only way the migrants know how: crossing the Rio Grande and staking a claim on the future.

After a few years of following the path of the migrant labor economy to places like Georgia, South Carolina, and Florida, Pedro graduated from the backbreaking, poorly paid work of the fields to a backbreaking, relatively better-paid job in a meatpacking plant in Garden City, Kansas, 1,200 miles from the Floreses' hometown of Cueramaro, Guanajuato. Pedro spoke no English, carried no "papers"—immigration documents which, in the era of the global, approximate a kind of safe-conduct pass to avoid stepping into the war zone that is much of the 2,000-mile-long border. But lacking papers neither dissuades Mexicans from migrating, nor discourages employers from hiring them. The meatpacking industry has grown in direct proportion to the increase of the population overall; Americans must have their burgers. It has been and continues to be a labor-intensive operation. Technology has transformed many sectors of the American workplace, but there has yet to be a virtual form of killing a 1,000-pound steer, skinning it, quartering it, eviscerating and boning it, washing its gizzards, crushing its bones into meal, and packing its choice cuts off to the wholesaler. Meatpacking, like other industries where the strength of the human body is irreplaceable—say, harvesting strawberries—has become an unpopular job for "native" Americans. The traditional sources of labor dried up: most African Americans and poor whites left rural jobs more than a generation ago. White college kids once worked summers in the fields, but no more: they know that the pay at a restaurant or mall shop is often higher and that those tasks do not take a terrible toll on the body. Visit just about any meatpacking warehouse in this country, and you'll find a workforce made up of people a lot like Pedro Flores.

As solitary as life can be for a Mexican man on the migrant road, so it is for the family he leaves behind in the *pueblo*, for the wife without a husband for the better part of the year, for children without their father. For thirteen years, Pedro lived and worked in Garden City the better part of each year, returning home only for visits of a week or two once every six months.

"I can't even keep track of how long he's been away from us," says Ventura Flores, wiping a tear away. "Imagine adding up all those days, weeks, months, and years! It is surely a long, long time."

As hard as Pedro worked at the meatpacking plant, so too did Ventura, raising six children like a single mother, albeit with the help of her husband's monthly checks from the States. She never left the *pueblo* during those thirteen years—she had never, ever left the *pueblo*, in fact— and yet at the end of that time, she was as exhausted as Pedro was, as if she'd logged every mile of road alongside him, matched him hour-for-hour working at the plant.

"I don't want my father to work double shifts anymore," Nora, the Floreses' eldest daughter still at home, says. "And my mother needs rest. She has worked so hard for all of us."

::

After another stint of several months' work in a Garden City meat plant, Pedro Flores travels back to Cueramero, Guanajuato. He boards a jet that takes him to the capital of the state, and then a taxi for the ride to the *pueblo*. It is twilight when he arrives, a scrim of cobalt in the eastern sky sweeping toward the last of the sun's orange-gold fire in the west. The arid plains of Guanajuato, dotted with nopal cactus, make for sunsets not unlike those the Floreses will see from the trailer park in Mecca, but they have no idea that they will be living and working in California a year from now. The migrant road is often an unpredictable path. I've known families who dreamed of living in Los Angeles only to flee the City of Angels for a heartland town when their children were lured into the typical urban ills of gangs and drugs. The economy itself is responsible for much of the migrants' peripatetic life. A downturn on the West Coast leads them to the Midwest; layoffs in the Midwest lead them to the East. Migrant farmworkers, of course, move with the crops: Spring can be a stint in the strawberry fields of Northern California and early summer lettuce in Missouri; late summer brings tobacco in North Carolina or apples in Washington; in wintertime, the perennial citrus groves of Florida and California.

Pedro's homecoming, as always, is a joyous one. Every member of his family rushes him with hugs and kisses as the taxi pulls up at the modest ranch house: his wife, Ventura, his children Nora, Lorena, Juana, Maribel, Pedro Jr., and Juliana, and his father, Bernal, who everyone calls "Papa Berna." Ventura immediately sets to preparing a meal of the kind Pedro hasn't tasted since the last time he was home. It is simple fare of *nopalitos* (cactus), beans, and tortillas, but to eat at the table surrounded by family immeasurably sweetens the meal.

It's been thirteen years of such homecomings. Pedro's children have grown up mostly in his absence. Nora was five years old when Pedro began his journeys north; she is now seventeen. He has missed her transition from little girl to adolescent to young woman, as he has most of the milestones of his younger children, their first steps and first words, their missing teeth and scraped knees, their ecstatic and painful awakenings to the world.

"It's been a long wait and I'm really tired of being alone," Pedro says. "[Ventura] tells me look, 'We're not happy when you're over there and we're here.' Together even if we only had beans and *nopalitos*. . . ." It wouldn't matter what was on the table, as long as they were together.

God and the government of the United States of America willing, it won't be much longer till the family is together year-round. Pedro has secured legal residency in the U.S., and become eligible to apply for visas on behalf of his family, a painfully slow bureaucratic process he began seven years ago. Finally, it appears that almost all is in order. There are only a few more forms to fill out, and an interview with an immigration officer. All so that his wife and children don't have to cross into America like Pedro did—illegally. Thirteen years of work and separation, all for this one chance at crossing a simple line on a map.

And what complications such lines can cause. Immigration statutes allow Pedro to sponsor only his unmarried children under the age of eighteen, which means they must complete the process in the next few months before Nora's birthday. His eldest daughter, Herminia, is twenty-three years old and married. For now, she will not be able to join the family in America. Papa Berna is not considered immediate family; he will have to try to secure a visa on his own. The old man is in his eighties now, still in relatively good health, but everyone knows the significance of his failing to get a visa: the likelihood that the family patriarch will die in Mexico, with most of his loved ones more than a thousand miles away.

Papa Berna says he doesn't want to cause any more bureaucratic headaches for the rest of the clan, but Pedro insists that everyone will remain together. It's what he's been working for all these years. "We want you to be there with us," Pedro tells his father. "I'm not going to leave you behind."

"I'd be of no use over there," the old man says.

"What do you mean you'd be of no use?" Pedro replies. "No one is useless! We already agreed, all go or none of us go."

Papa Berna finally admits to his true desire. "I've been sad and lonely since [my wife died]. I'll be even lonelier when they leave."

Now Pedro Jr. steps up and emulates his father. "We're taking you no matter what!"

::

Few people in the Third World leave their homes on a whim; migration is no American-style joyride. There are dangers on the road to the Promised Land. Unscrupulous smugglers, harrowing illegal journeys through rugged terrain, the trauma of family separation, the sting of discrimination, the bewildering encounter with a foreign tongue and mores, labor conditions ripe for accidents and illness and even death. To leave one's homeland, there must be an imperative: some force casts you out of Eden: an underdeveloped economy, famine, dictatorship.

The Flores family works a slice of land on an *ejido*, communal property that is the legacy of the Mexican Revolution's attempt at a redistribution of wealth. But a series of changes, natural and manmade, have dealt a harsh blow to Mexico's rural economy. The North American Free Trade Agreement (NAFTA) slashed government subsidies for such staples as corn—the lifeblood of the Mexican small farm. What good is a parcel when there isn't enough money to buy seeds, fertilizer, and pesticides to avoid a plague that makes an entire year's work for naught? Water rights in the region have been gradually usurped by large private landholders, leaving the crops at nature's mercy. Persistent drought conditions over the last several years throughout central and northern Mexico have created nearly dust-bowl conditions. Some sociologists think that the appearance in the mid-1990s of the *chupacabras*, a Big Foot–like bogeyman that mysteriously supposedly attacked farm animals at night, sucking their blood like a vampire, is a sign of a collective rural unconscious terrified by sudden and traumatic change.

One morning Papa Berna and eight-year-old Pedro Jr. take a stroll across the family's parcel. Grandson rides atop an old nag while grandfather pulls the reins. Papa Berna's boots and the horse's hooves crunch

KARTEMQUIN FILMS

Pedro Flores, Jr. in Cueramero

through a field of brittle, stunted corn. The sky is dusty, but cloudless. There is nary a hint of rain on the horizon.

Pedrito asks Papa Berna why the harvest yields so little. Pedro is too young to recall when the wet season brought enough rain to bring the now-fallow land to life, but he's heard his elders speak of the old days.

Yes, there used to be a grand harvest, grandfather says. The rains came in the summer months. Towering cottony clouds with heavy gray bellies would magically appear and the drops fell, beautiful generous tears from a merciful God. The first rain of the season came down on soil dusty from the long dry season; you'd see puffs of dry earth rise with each drop. Then the dust was gone, drowned by the water that formed rivulets and followed the contours of the furrowed land, soaking the seeds underneath. Such an intoxicating aroma there was then, especially at night, the perfume of moist, newly fertile earth. When the winds blew away the storm, the sky would turn a rich azure. An inch under the ground, the moistened seeds would cook as if in an incubator under the Tropic of Cancer sun. Soon came the morning that the baby shoots sprang forth across the land. The rain and sun alternated this way for the better part of five months, and the men of the fields carefully tended the shoots that became plants and bloomed fruit or grew vegetable roots. Nature and man worked in harmony, and everyone on the *ejido* would celebrate at harvest, offering God the first of the bounty of beans and corn with fiestas and masses in the church.

But then the rains came later every year and fell less frequently. It reminded Papa Berna of how things were when he was Pedrito's age. The brutal dictator Porfirio Díaz doggedly held absolute power for thirty years before the Revolution, which ended the year Papa Berna was born, 1917. Under Díaz's reign, the *hacendados*, wealthy landowners, controlled every inch of arable land. There was famine then, not from a plague of insects or a crop-killing fungus, but the manmade kind: the nation's breadbasket fed only the rich and government soldiers or went to export.

Why didn't the government just give people the food they needed to survive, little Pedro wonders, swaying to the nag's gentle gait through the field.

Because the government *was* the *hacendados*, Papa Berna says. People starved to death not because there was no food, but because it wasn't given to them. The government, *el mal gobierno*, as the Zapatistas and other revolutionaries of the time called it, stole everything. Things got so bad that people died of hunger on the very land they sowed and reaped. Papa Berna remembers the bodies, sacks of bones, being buried almost daily.

Where, Papa Berna? Pedrito asks.

Right here, Papa Berna says. Right here on this land we're walking on right now. Not so much as a coffin—who could afford one? And no priest to say a prayer. There were simply too many dead; they were buried where they fell. Beneath this land of ours lie the bones of our ancestors, reminding us of the way things once were. They remind us so that it may never happen again.

The dead corn stalks rustle in the breeze. Perhaps, Pedrito imagines, it is sound of the bones of the dead chafing together below the earth.

But who knows, Papa Berna says. Who knows if it'll happen again. Maybe it's starting to happen again, right here, right now.

No one knows if and when the rains will return. But one thing is certain: the Mexican and American governments' promises of prosperity on both sides of the border with the implementation of NAFTA have gone unfulfilled. The rural economy is in free fall, a way of life disappearing. Over the course of four generations, the Flores family will have gone from working land that was once owned by the *hacendados* and then deeded back to them by the Revolution, only to see the parcel go fallow and eventually wind up back in the hands of big landowners, forcing them to abandon their patrimony for the picking fields of California, whose land was once worked by Indians, then Mexicans, then cowboys, and now the faceless multinational corporations that will turn profits on the backs of the Floreses and their cheap labor.

::

It is time for Pedro to return to Kansas. He prays that it will be the last time he departs this way, alone. Soon, there will be an appointment with American immigration authorities in Juárez, Chihuahua, just across the Rio Grande from El Paso, Texas. It has taken the family seven years to prepare to cross the line legally. But first, Pedro must go back to work. He cannot afford to be fired for taking too much time off at the meat-packing plant, especially now, when he has to save every penny for the fees that the American authorities charge for processing visa applications—several thousand dollars.

And so comes the *despedida*, the agonizing farewell. A few days earlier, Ventura was unpacking her husband's small suitcase and now she is filling it again, carefully folding the clothes as she wipes away her tears. Soon, a taxi is waiting in front of the Floreses' one-room ranch house. Pedro's wife and children huddle by him, everyone crying softly, except little Pedro, who wails loudly. Father scoops son into his arms. "You behave like a real man," he tells him. "Don't start worrying or crying for silly reasons. Right now is no time to cry."

This macho tack does not alleviate little Pedro's jags in the least, so Pedro Sr. tries a lighter touch.

"We're not saying good-bye, we're saying *hasta luego*." Now he plays Schwarzenegger: "We're saying, '*hasta la vista*, baby.' If you're going to learn English over there, it's time to start now."

Pedrito quiets down a bit. But now father must become son before his own father. Pedro approaches Papa Berna. The men, separated by several decades, are cut from the same provincial cloth. Both wear the ubiquitous cowboy hat of the Mexican countryside, jeans and braided belts with big, ornate buckles, and boots. Three generations of Flores men have worked the land of Cueramero. The family's hold on the land will end with this generation, its earth and crops and *animalitos* will soon become a dimming memory for Pedro's children, and exist only as legend for his children's children.

Pedro and Papa Berna hesitate before one another, two men at a loss in such emotional encounters. When they finally embrace stiffly—standing side by side, arms clapping each other's shoulders—there is in their contact a century's worth of struggle to retain the family's place in the world, and now the world is undoing their very history, to begin a new one: In the lives of migrants, history tends to erase history. Pedro bows his head before his father. The old man raises his hand and whispers a prayer, blessing his son for a safe and successful journey—one that the patriarch can barely comprehend. Papa Berna was born only a few years after the Wright brothers floated their flying machine for a few precious seconds above the grassy knolls of Kitty Hawk; in a couple of hours, his son will board a Boeing jet and cross the great Mexican desert—interminable by bus or train and unthinkable on horseback. The land will scroll beneath him rapidly, its impoverished *ejidos* and alluvial fans, the burgeoning industrial towns of the north and the muddy snake called the Rio Grande (known to Mexicans as the Río Bravo, the raging river), and then the anally planned avenues and redundant suburban tracts of the cities in the States, the dusty, oily flats of Texas, the gleaming towers of emerald cities, the endless furrowed land of the Great Plains.

The ritual done, Pedro turns away from his father, who is trembling with emotion. If it weren't for the tears welling in Pedro's eyes, it would look like there was a frozen half-smile on his face. It's just the muscles of his cheeks trying mightily to hold back his pain.

::

It is a couple of weeks before Christmas in Ciudad Juárez. In a city that bakes in dusty heat during the summer months, the winds from the north now blow cold. The Flores clan—Pedro, Ventura, Nora, Lorena, Juana, Maribel, Pedro Jr., and Juliana—have made the trek via bus from their *pueblo*. The only missing members are Papa Berna and daughter Herminia. For the moment, there is no way for either to secure a visa.

The bus station is a gleaming citadel under the acrid industrial sky of Juárez. Its ceiling is so high that it is a sky unto itself, the arriving and departing passengers on ground level dwarfed by the mammoth structure. But in Mexico, the postmodern and premodern often occupy the same space. The Floreses, walking together in a tight unit, walk up to a shrine to the Virgin of Guadalupe, Mexico's patroness and object of more prayers and petitions than even Jesus Christ. She is encased in glass, haloed with blinking colored lights, fresh flowers at her feet. Pedro doffs his hat and bows his head. The children gaze reverentially at her serene countenance. *Dearest little Virgin, we ask you to guide us safely across the border, may the Americans receive us without a hitch. . . .*

Now the Floreses stand across a wide boulevard from the American Consulate, a building designed, as all other American consulates around the world, more like a military compound than a diplomatic station. No replica of the Statue of Liberty here, no benevolent greeting to the "huddled masses yearning to breathe free." From the Mexican point of view, the bunker must be bewildering. What do the Americans fear from us, who cross the line merely to work, seeking *la vida major*, the American dream itself?

The brood waits for a break in the torrent of traffic. Juárez–El Paso is one of the busiest international gateways in the world. Under NAFTA, the flow over the bridge that spans the Rio Grande has become a flood. Trucks crammed with goods head both north and south. Raw materials for appliances, cars, video games, stereo components, toys, clothes cross into Mexico, are assembled into finished products at *maquiladoras*, and then cross back over into the States. Mexican strawberries head north, American corn—yet another blow to the Mexican small farmer—goes south.

It seems as if the border is no more; wall has become sieve. And yet the border remains very real when it comes to the movement of people over the line. Americans cross easily into Mexico, of course, the immigration officials waving them through toward the dog races, red-light districts, and bars that don't "card" gringo teens. On the other side, American immigration and customs officials grill every dark-skinned person, poring over their passports and visas and work permits, searching luggage and strip-searching bodies for contraband. It's not exactly the West Bank, but the line between the U.S. and Mexico is clearly a militarized zone. It is also one of the most absurd borders in the world. Americans hire undocumented Latin American workers in practically every sector of the economy and in every region of the country, but then enact public policy that seeks to deport "illegals" and fortify the border to prevent them from crossing the line in the first place. The Flores family has taken all this to heart. They will play by Uncle Sam's bizarre rules.

The Flores kids are wide-eyed in awe of the Big City. Ventura is wide-eyed, too, but with what looks like sheer terror. Pedro is grim-faced, focused on navigating not just the traffic but also the gauntlet of American visa bureaucracy. Every ounce of energy he's poured into picking crops, working construction jobs, and manning the boning line at the meatpacking plant in Garden City has come down to this moment.

"What I want to give [my family] is like an inheritance for them," he says. "I have nothing else to leave them other than these [visas] so that they can cross, so that they'll be able to say that I left them with something."

The Flores family at the border

Like so many aspects of the migrant life, applying for visas, even if one is eligible under the law, is a gamble. A simple mistake on one of the endless forms can mean a delay of months, years. Running afoul of the law in the States, even for a minor offense, can disqualify you for life for visas or residency. It also takes money to the play the game, the one thing that most Mexicans don't have. Pedro calculated the total budget to get the family into the U.S. at $5,000. Bus fare for Pedro to return home to Cueramero so the entire family could travel together to Juárez: $140. Then $325 for each family member's Mexican passport, without which they'd be in trouble with both Mexican and American authorities. Identification photos, $28. Medical exams for everyone, another American visa requisite, $460. They must pay $1,820 to the American

Consulate in application fees. And $1,740 for motel, food, and new shoes for the kids.

When Pedro arrived in Cueramero, he'd saved $2,400 from his earnings in Garden City, $2,600 short of his goal. Americans often wonder how immigrants produce such sums of money—a family member working in the States can't do it on his own, as Pedro's case makes clear. With the state of the Mexican rural economy, there is little or no contribution from work on the other side of the border. And yet an illegal crossing is even more expensive than attempting a legal one—and more Mexicans gain entry to the States via smuggler than with a visa. Smugglers these days charge up to $2,000 a head. If the Floreses were to cross with a "coyote," as the smugglers are called, they'd need around $16,000. And many of Mexico's poorest citizens routinely come up with such sums. The money comes from Mexico, after all, not from a worker's pitiable wages but from moneylenders, an essential black market proletarian niche in the transnational economy.

The Floreses borrowed the balance of their projected budget from a loan shark in Guanajuato. A portion of the principal plus $300 in interest is to be paid back every month—which the Floreses will be able to do, with no little sacrifice, once they establish themselves in the States. When Pedro and Ventura visited the loan shark's house, the old woman counted out about half the sum in American dollars, and then produced a check for the rest. Ventura had never seen so much cash in her life. The sight bothered her so much that she had to turn away as the bills piled up in her husband's hand.

The first order of business is for Pedro to stop by a money-changing office to cash the check from the moneylender in Guanajuato. Ventura is scared that the check, being from the provinces, will not be honored here in the city. Ventura and kids wait across the street while Pedro enters the office. Mom's anxiety passes along to the kids. The longer

Pedro is away, the more nervous they become, crossing their fingers, whispering prayers to the Virgin. When he finally appears—his face emotionless—mom and kids hold their breath. The check was cashed. *Thank you, little Virgin. . . .*

"We're one step closer to victory!" Pedro exults.

"Give me five, Dad!" says Nora, and they slap hands.

The family stays in a rundown border motel the night before their appointment at the consulate. There are still a few *i*'s to dot and *t*'s to cross in the paperwork. When it comes time for Ventura to sign her name, her pent-up anxieties finally explode. Ventura is illiterate, and Pedro is holding the pen out to her, coaxing her to scribble something, anything, on the form.

"I'm telling you I can't do it!" she snaps at Pedro.

Later, in the hallway outside their room, Pedro tries to give his wife a pep talk. Ventura stands with head bowed and hands folded below her belly. She is ashamed and terrified. She is farther from home than she's ever been in her entire life.

::

The colors of Christmas flash and blink all over Juárez, in larger-than-life nativities, on trees and buildings festooned with foil and strings of lights. Street vendors offer holiday sweets and beverages and in the *colonias*, the working-class neighborhoods, residents perform the age-old ritual of the *posadas*, processions reenacting Joseph and Mary's search for lodging in Bethlehem. Venus hangs low and bright in the desert sky, the evening star leading the pilgrims to the manger. The Floreses do not attend any *posadas*; they have no relatives here. In fact, they don't know a single person in Juárez. Their version of the *posadas* is a trip to the American Consulate.

Pedro has all the relevant documents inside a canary yellow plastic folder bound with a drawstring. At the guard gate, he fishes for the appointment pass, and the Marine waves the family in. The Floreses wait in a large hall with perhaps 250 seats, only about a third of which are occupied. Ventura continues to wear her emotions on her sleeve; she sits rigidly, eyes fixed on the windows behind which sit the immigration officers. Even Pedro shows a little of his anxiety now, his cheerleading banter now quieted. Did he fill out the forms correctly? Will the immigration officer be in a foul mood? Will she speak in English and make things all the harder for him? *Dearest Virgin . . .*

The Floreses' name is called out through the loudspeakers.

The immigration officer is neither pleasant nor pissed off, she just *is*, performing the same task she does every day, poring over the same exact forms, a peasant family waiting expectantly on the other side of the glass. Pedro hands over his paperwork.

"You have only one sponsor for the whole family?" she asks. Pedro nods. The most crucial requisite for the Floreses' visas is to have an American citizen vouch on their behalf that he will help them get settled in the States and, theoretically, serve as their economic safety net. Pedro's cousin Ernestino Ortega offered himself up for the role. But there is one problem.

"Mr. Ortega qualifies three people," the officer says, naming Ventura, Maribel, and Juliana. "We can give them their visas today."

The crushing news is that the other four—Pedrito, Nora, Lorena, and Juana do not qualify. They will need their own sponsor. Pedro is informed that the Consulate closes for the Christmas holiday in three days. The Floreses have seventy-two hours to find a sponsor—a seemingly impossible task. Ventura's worst fears are confirmed.

Stunned, the family sits back down in the waiting room.

"My mind is racing now," Pedro says. "Who could I leave behind? As a last resort I could leave [Pedrito], he's so young. I could resolve his case later and come back for him."

Apparently, Pedrito hears something of this comment. Suddenly he bursts into tears.

"Don't go over there without me," he sobs. "You're all going over there and you're not going to take me."

"No, no one is going to stay behind," Pedro Sr. says. "We're all going to go; don't cry anymore. We won't leave you behind. You'll help me support the family. Do you think I'd leave you behind? Papa Berna will come, too. Dry your eyes. . . ."

Across the street from the consulate, the family works a pay phone. Pedro calls a co-worker, Ventura a relative. Neither can offer themselves as sponsors. Just as it's looking like all is lost, Pedro rings Bernadina Franco, a co-worker in Kansas. He pleads his case. Bernadina has nothing to gain from offering herself as a sponsor, but she's seen Pedro tirelessly laboring at the meat plant with only one goal in mind: to reunite his family. She agrees to sponsor the rest of the family.

It is a season of miracles after all.

::

Ventura did not take well to the relative comfort of life in Kansas. She did not work at the meatpacking plant, and she found herself mostly bored at home, without nearly as many chores as she had back home in the rural setting.

Today, she works alongside her husband at a greenhouse nursery in Mecca and it seems as if a measure of her self-worth has returned. She is working again, her body aching in the early evening as she returns home and resumes work at home to stand alongside Irma in the kitchen and cook and clean and mind her children. When she finally sits down to watch TV, she is so tired that she begins dozing off almost immediately. She is in bed by ten almost every night, except Saturday, when the adults get off work a little earlier than usual and splurge a bit by eating a choicer cut of meat with their usual dose of beans and tortillas. The mood on Saturday night is festive in the trailer park, the music louder. Some of the men drink a bit and whoop it up. Still, it is a modest fiesta, not at all like back home. Nothing here is like back home, say the adults with a sigh. Nora and Lorena, the teenage children, who emigrated too late to learn English and acculturate fully, tend to agree; sometimes it is harder for a teenage migrant to imagine a future in America than it is for their parents, who are so invested in the goal of *la vida major* for their children. The younger ones can learn the language rapidly. While the adults are in the fields, the kids spend eight hours in a public school where the teachers speak only in English. Theirs will be a Mexican-American existence, roots firmly planted on this side of the border; on journeys back to the *pueblo,* they will feel out of place as much as the older kids and adults feel at home. The parents themselves usually never get beyond halting English. Pedro, after fifteen years of commuting between the States and Guanajuato, can barely get by, relying on co-workers who speak better English than he. In later years, Pedro and Ventura will speak to their younger children and hear them respond with the sharp consonants of the foreign tongue. There will surely be rows over what is and is not acceptable of the new mores the kids learn—children growing up in the "liberal" north, they will expect to go out at night without chaperones. They may consider leaving home when they turn eighteen. They may talk of going to college. There may be a clash between American individualism and Old World notions of family and community and maybe no way to bridge the divide. There are not a few

Ventura Flores at work in Mecca

immigrant parents who after years of hard work and sacrifice wonder if it was all worth it when they can no longer comprehend their children.

It must be the loneliest of feelings for an immigrant parent to watch a child be swallowed up by America. *Solo.*

::

By day, Ventura and Pedro work just up the road from the trailer park in the greenhouse nursery. In the summer months, the temperatures in the California desert often rise above 110 degrees and the relative humidity inside the nursery is near 100 percent. Ventura's sister Irma and her daughter Lorena work the fields. It is hard for outsiders to imagine green orchards surrounding this forlorn town on the edge of the Salton Sea, which sits some 300 feet below sea level, one of the lowest points in the United States. But there is plenty of water here. The California Aqueduct channels it from the Colorado River, and it streams across the fields of citrus, dates, strawberries, cauliflower, and lettuce. Growing consumer demand, engineering brilliance, and a pliable, low-wage labor force have turned the desert into an oasis.

But it is no paradise in the greenhouse nurseries or in the picking fields. Ventura's mother and her sister Irma were the first to arrive in Mecca nearly twenty years ago. Irma began working the fields in her teens—she did not finish school—and has remained there ever since. Not surprisingly, she constantly reminds her children that they must be diligent students.

"Only through education will they be able to avoid working like I have all my life," she says. "I have no choice. How can I get a job that pays well when I speak no English?"

How many times I've heard "Americans" complain about people much like Irma. "They come here and just don't want to learn the language," they say to me since, I suppose, they consider me a "representative" of "my people." I am only the son and grandson of immigrants, and so I cannot speak as an immigrant, but this much I know: I've never met a migrant who didn't want to learn English. Some who arrive in this country in later years simply cannot—especially if they never learned to read and write Spanish in the first place (they don't need English classes—they need a literacy program). Other adult migrants arrive here with a basic level of education, but find themselves so worn down by their jobs and child-rearing responsibilities that they simply don't have the energy to attend night school. Even those migrants who do have the wherewithal to learn often find public language classes past capacity and cannot afford private tutoring. In this sense, they are no different than the Italians, Jews, and Poles who arrived on American shores a couple of generations ago:

those who arrived as mature adults lived out their lives speaking the maternal tongue, placing their children in the difficult position of inter-locutors for even the most basic errands and paperwork, decoding not just language but the norms and mores of their new country.

What is different about Mexicans living and working in the States is that, unique among immigrants in America, their Old World home actu-ally borders the New, adding a layer of suspicion: Can Mexicans really be trusted? The lands of the South have always loomed darkly in the American imagination, what with revolutionaries, Catholicism, and, in recent times, the specter of drug trafficking. And more: the border between the United States in Mexico is, by and large, a porous one. The majority of "illegal" immigrants in this country are from Mexico. There are illegal Irish, Australians, and Brits among us, too, but we don't rail against them. The Mexicans are the most visible sign that, as the anti-immigrant lobby says, our "sovereignty is under attack." In the post-9/11 world, such ideas carry a much more sinister tone. To make matters worse, many Latin Americans have facial features similar to Arabs—a point of older immigration history in that the Moors conquered Spain in medieval times and thus when the Spaniards arrived in the New World, Arab blood came with them. A young Mexican man was attacked on a California freeway not long after the terror attacks by a crew of whites seeking revenge. He was mistaken for an Arab.

If you sit down with Irma and Ventura and the kids out in the dusty expanse of the California desert, it is impossible to match the paranoid images of Mexican immigrants promoted by xenophobes and fanned by the media. Irma and Ventura just want what every immigrant who's come to America wants. They are invoking the American creed: that immigrant elders sacrifice their very bodies in labor for the sake of the next generation. And yet if you do get to know this family, it is hard to imagine that the sacrifice will achieve its desired goal. The jobs they hold take too terrible a toll on their bodies, and the slim paychecks do not translate into anything more than subsistence—a life not that much different than what they had back home in Guanajuato. Right now, in the middle of this brutal summer, it is hard to believe that the Floreses will ever find a way out of the desert and leave behind the hell-on-earth that is Mecca.

But I'm an outsider looking in, and I've been around immigrants enough to know that I'm probably projecting my own ambitions upon them. The only way for the Floreses to endure is to imagine the future. Even in Mecca, they dream their dreams.

The Narrative of Exile :: **Los Tigres del Norte and Manu Chao**

I have heard Los Tigres del Norte on so many occasions, in so many different places over the years – live in concert in a dusty rodeo ring, on a battered boom box in the picking fields, blasting from car stereo speakers in the migrant barrios from California to North Carolina, covered by street musicians in the city and in the provinces, in cantinas north and south of the border – that I cannot recall the first time my ears perked up to their infectious norteño style, their absolutely idiosyncratic vocals (a nasally, slightly off-key delivery delivered with great bravado), their inimitable polka-inflected accordion riffs. Theirs is an omnipresent soundtrack on the migrant trail. In the realm of Mexican pop, Los Tigres del Norte are as ubiquitous as the Virgin of Guadalupe, Mexico's patroness. Come to think of it, wherever She appears, the Tigers of the North cannot be far behind – or vice versa. Their music is the ultimate soundtrack for migrant Mexico, for every man, woman and child hurtling across the land in search of *la vida mejor*.

Much has been written in recent years about the *narco-corrido* genre in the American press. Los Tigres were playing odes to infamous drug traffickers long before the gringos took note, Robin Hood tales of good guys gone bad and bad guys leaning good within a world ruled by payback and the code of honor in Mexico's northern territories, the dusty expanses where drug cartels not only bribe authorities, but become Authority itself. American critics see in the *narco-corrido* a corollary to gangsta rap – and a Mexican nationalist slap to the U.S. War on Drugs. All true enough. What they rarely write about is the how deeply imbedded the genre is in the Mexican psyche, and how the *narco* prefix is merely the latest in over a century's worth of popular odes exploring Mexican outlaw-ness. During the days of the Revolution, the *corrido*, or ballad, was a form of street communication that celebrated the exploits of rebel leaders in their struggle against the army of dictator Porfirio Díaz, the Augusto Pinochet of his time. Like Dylan pointing to that hard rain about to fall, the *corrido* singers, traveling troubadours, sensed history as it was being made and nudged it along, without the help of radio or phonograph. The *corrido* was more than a mirror for the Revolution; it was an integral part of the Revolution itself.

Migration across the U.S.-Mexico border predates the Revolution, and its narrative was present at the turn of the twentieth century in Mexican popular song. "Canción mixteca," penned by José López Alavés in 1912, told of the heartbreak of a Mexican far from home:

Qué lejos estoy del suelo donde he nacido
intense nostalgia invade mi pensamiento
al verme tan solo y triste, cual hoja al viento
¡Quisiera llorar, quisiera morir, de sentimiento!

(How far I am from the land where I was born
an intense nostalgia takes hold of my thoughts
now that I'm so alone and sad, like a leaf on the wind
I'd like to cry, I'd like to die, from this feeling!)

While it is probable that Alavés was writing about his own internal migration – from his provincial hometown in Oaxaca to Mexico City, where he studied at the National Conservatory – "Canción mixteca" has become Mexico's migrant anthem, a song that every Mexican, on both sides of the border, knows by heart. But it is on the north side of the Rio Grande that the song becomes most poignant. Recently, I sang the tune in Jackson Hole, Wyoming, performing for an audience composed largely of Mexicans living and working in the resort town's hotels and restaurants. (Imagine, Mexicans in Wyoming, shivering in the cold wind blowing down from the Tetons – how much farther from home can one get?) I often sing with my eyes closed, but on this occasion I heard whispers coming from the crowd, and I opened them to see dozens of migrants, sighing every word along with me. Tears rolled down the cheeks of a grandmother sitting in the front row as her voice cracked along to the winsome melody. The song summoned the homeland in their hearts and transformed Jackson Hole not just into a Little Mexico, but Mexico itself.

Los Tigres institutionalized the migrant *corrido* in the 1970s and 1980s, praising the adventures of the *mojados* (the Spanish translation of "wetbacks," which in the migrant lexicon is a badge of honor rather than the nasty epithet it is in English) and hoisting a banner that they carry to this day, one that declares workers on the northern side of the border to be every bit as Mexican as anyone who's never left the *pueblo*. In the Tigres's ballads, migrants face off with vicious agents of the *migra* (Border Patrol), abusive gringo *patrones* (bosses), flirt with ravishing American blondes, and always, always dream of returning to the homeland as *mojado* – heroes who'll live out their last days in the *pueblo* in high style. And yet, despite the Tigres's earnest nationalism, they are no cultural essentialists. Their migrant protagonists speak Spanglish (thus defending the so-called *pochos* – the Mexicans who speak a patois of Spanish and English – from attacks that they've sold out to gringo culture), indulge the influence of American pop, can even become citizens of the U.S. – the Tigres actually urge them to, so as to have a political voice in their second home – all without forsaking the homeland. For Los Tigres, the border is less a wall than a sieve, and Mexico less a geographical place than a metaphysical space defined by those thrown northward by the sputtering economy of the south and the labor-hungry north.

The band's history is a migrant tale unto itself. Natives of the northern Mexican state of Sinaloa, they performed their first gig in the States – a Mexican Independence Day parade in San Jose, California, on September 16, 1968 – when the oldest member was still only fourteen years old. When they arrived at *la garita*, the border crossing gate in Tijuana, a Customs officer peeked into the car and called them "little tigers." And so Los Tigres del Norte were born on the very border that they've spent the last thirty-five years chronicling. An added transcultural twist to their story is that the promoter who brought the band across the border was himself an immigrant – from, of all places, Manchester, England. Art Walker knew not a word of Spanish, nor Los Tigres a word of English, but that didn't prevent the business partners from starting up a collaboration that would transform the band into an international phenomenon, with some thirty albums to date.

The band members never returned to live full-time in Mexico after that first gig in San Jose, and they remain Northern California residents to this day (they have not yet, as they have urged their fans to do, become naturalized citizens), a fact that makes their success south of the border all the more peculiar. Throughout most of the twentieth century, pop culture flowed back and forth across the border through clear-cut channels: American pop went south to inspire wannabe gringo fads, and Mexican pop went north to stoke the cultural hearth of migrants on the long and winding road. But Los Tigres turned the experience of Mexican pop upside down: Living in the states and chronicling the migrant experience, they exported their brand of Mexican-ness to Mexico.

One of their earliest migrant ballad hits flies in the face of any illusions prospective migrants might have about America:

Aquí estoy establecido
En los Estados Unidos.
Diez años pasaron ya
En que cruzé de mojado
Sigo siendo un ilegal . . .

¿De qué me sirve el dinero
Si estoy como prisionero?

Cuando me acuerdo hasta lloro
Aunque la jaula sea de oro,
No deja de ser prisión.

(I've made my home
In the United States.
Ten years have gone by
Since I crossed as a wetback
But I'm still an illegal . . .

What good is money
If I'm living like a prisoner?
When I remember home I cry
Even if this cage is made of gold,
It's still a prison.)

    – "Jaula de oro" (Golden Cage)

The myth of streets paved with gold turns out to be a prison both existentially and in the discrimination the undocumented endure in their adopted homeland. And prison it is. The migrant can't easily return home: In the first place, there's the matter of money (the reason he came to America in the first place). But there's also the fact that even a physical return home will not satisfy the migrant's desire to feel at home; the homeland, frozen in the time of the migrant mind, no longer exists. The first-generation migrant is trapped between past and future in a bewildering present, cut off from *pueblo* history and, tragically, from his own children, who, if born in the States, will wind up speaking better English than Spanish. (And if the children are back home, he is the one who will be foreign before them.)

For years, the Tigres performed mostly in migrant barrios and "sender" communities back home, existing in commercial ignominy. But the underground phenomenon was so pervasive that eventually the Mexico music industry powers-that-be had no choice but to back what was already a huge word-of-mouth sensation. The Tigres were signed by Fonovisa, the music division of Mexico's largest media conglomerate, Televisa – and suddenly the band was being produced and presented by the very Mexico City–based elites that had considered them, and most northern Mexican music for that matter, to be the crass beat of the dusty provinces. (In the Byzantine world of global capital, Fonovisa was eventually sold to American-based media conglomerate Univision, which had itself once been owned by Televisa.) And yet, there are few who would decry Los Tigres as "sellouts." Dozens of albums into their career, they continue churning out lyrics and beats that capture the joys and sorrows of Mexico's people of perpetual motion, updating the mise-en-scène as necessary. The band continues to ruffle feathers with its insistence on glorifying the "illegal" side of Mexican life – an undocumented worker, a narco-trafficker – and the Mexican equivalents of Pat Robertson and the Christian Coalition continue to fulminate about their message. But such critiques are to no avail. They are among the few Mexican acts to deserve the overblown publicist's epithet of *los ídolos del pueblo*—the people's heroes.

On their stunning *Jefe de jefes* (Boss of Bosses) double-CD release of 1997, they included "El mojado acaudalado," a migrant epic that details the most recent movements of the migrant labor economy in the U.S.:

Adiós, adiós Colorado
Nevada, y Oregón.
Adiós les dice el mojado
Que se empapó de sudor
En los campos de Arizona
Fabricas de Nueva York . . .

. . . ya me pasié por Atlanta
Por Oklahoma también
Me decía una guera en Florida
"I love you, Mexican man."

(Good-bye, good-bye, Colorado,
Nevada, and Oregon.
Good-bye says the wetback
Who dripped with sweat
In the fields of Arizona
And factories of New York . . .

(. . . I've made my way through Atlanta
And even Oklahoma too
A white girl in Florida told me
"I love you, Mexican man.")

An ambitious concept album that features cover art of the band in magnificent pimping leather against the backdrop of the ruins of Alcatraz State Prison, *Jefe de jefes* also includes the wistful points-of-view of forlorn migrants realizing that their American dreams will never be realized, kamikaze narco-runners going out in a hail of bullets, and transfrontier love stories. The *telenovela*, the Mexican TV soap opera, is often regarded as the ultimate populist genre, but there's never been a soap that comes close to capturing the borderscapes depicted by Los Tigres. And yes, it's all danceable music, set to the $^3/_4$ polka beat left behind by German and Polish merchants who toured the northern regions of Mexico a century and a half ago.

Rock 'n' roll and rap have arrived in Mexico of late, and many a teen of both urb and province can delight to a Spanish-language vocal cutting across wailing guitars and the boom of a classic rock drum kit. But the northern *corrido* has not flagged in the least, and many a rocker pays homage by covering beloved Tigres tunes. After all, the migrant ballad is still being written by the millions of Mexicans who continue to cross the line between Mexico and the United States. As long as that is the case, and as long as they have the breath to belt out their *corridos*, in the Mexican narrative of exile, the Tigres will rule.

::

Solo voy con mi pena
Sola va mi condena
Correr es mi destino
Para burlar la ley
Perdido en el corazón
De la grande Babylon
Me dicen el clandestino
Por no llevar papel . . .

. . . Soy una raya en el mar
Fantasma en la ciudad
Mi vida va prohibida
Dice la autoridad . . .

(I travel alone with my woe
My punishment travels alone
My destiny is to be on the run
And make fools of the cops
Lost in the heart
Of a huge Babylon
They call me the clandestine one
Because I don't have any papers . . .

... I'm a streak of light across the sea
A ghost in the city
My life is proscribed
The authorities say ...)

From across the Atlantic comes another voice singing of the migrant road, a voice that sings in Spanish, English, Portuguese, and French, a voice belonging to a body born in France to parents from Spain, which body as a young man thrashed to the early punk and rockabilly beats of London. Manu Chao, founder and lead vocalist of the now-defunct Mano Negra, is often labeled "Latin alternative," but to my mind he offers a vision more of what "world beat" could be if it weren't for Americans and Europeans insisting on the consumption of exotic roots. An organic cultural chameleon, Manu also makes the likes of David Byrne and other First World pop artists who attempt syncretism sound facile by comparison. When Byrne tries on Afro-Cuban or Brazilian styles, he does so with the luxury of a Winona Ryder shoplifting at Saks – the sounds are torn from their historical moorings, and a colonial fiesta ensues. When someone like Manu arrives on the scene – steeped in Old World history as much as he was weaned on American and British pop – the result is altogether different.

On 1999's *Clandestino* – to this critic's ears, the ultimate musical masterpiece of the global era – Manu creates a seamless lyric universe so utterly diverse that it is impossible to locate it on any kind of cultural map. Swinging with gypsy soul, connected to Latin American beats, a diligent student of sampling technology and an accomplished poet, Manu's home is the eye of the global hurricane, his music reaching out to grab fragments of far-flung histories and fashioning from them a sublime – and deeply unsettling – pastiche. All the elements blend into one another, literally: There are no breaks between songs on the entire album, only cross-fades and immediate cuts forward. The final track, "El viento," sums up Manu's theme:

El viento viene
El viento se va
Por la carretera . . .
El hambre viene
El hombre se va
Sin mas razón
El hambre viene
El hombre se va
Ruta Babylon
Por la carretera . . .
¿Cuando volverá?

(The wind comes
The wind goes
Along the highway . . .
Hunger comes
And the man goes
That's the way it goes
Hunger comes
And the man goes
The route to Babylon
Along the highway . . .
When will he return?)
     – "El viento" (The Wind)

The wind is the economy of transnational corporate power, and it blows masses of migrants on a long march along a road with no beginning or end. Samples on the track include what sounds like a dinner party of music industry types at Spago's. A church bell rings madly in the distance. Against the forlorn vocal – accompanied by a single, brittle guitar strumming a spare reggae

– it paints a picture in my mind of those garish bourgeois figures Diego Rivera painted above desperate Indian paupers hoping for a crust of bread. The song ends with Manu repeating "along the highway . . . along the highway . . ." with the rush and howl of wind swallowing up his vocal, his guitar, the dinner party, the desperate migrants.

Clandestino is an ode to refugees from civil wars and dictatorships and natural disasters, to the Chinese undocumented worker in Tokyo and the Indian techie in Silicon Valley, to the sex workers serving European tourists in Thailand, to the ones who've already left, to the ones who have yet to return, to the ones who languish in Los Tigres' *jaula de oro.*

When I think of Ventura Flores sitting on the stoop of her stifling trailer in Mecca, I think of Manu's terrible wind, of how it picked her up and dropped her in the middle of nowhere, and of how she waits even now for the wind to come again.

5 :: India to Silicon Valley ::
Anjan Bacchu and Harshini Radhakrishnan

Anjan and Harshini

::

IT IS A LONG-RUNNING ARGUMENT BETWEEN FATHER AND SON. FATHER SPEAKS of the past; and son, the future. Son speaks of individual freedom; and father, of contributing to the greater good. Father believes that cultivating the mind and the spirit is the only meaningful path in life; son is ambitious about career and has a taste for consumer culture. Much of the son's life is spent writing the forward-slashes and equal signs of computer code, the evanescent text of the virtual realm. Father believes only in the text that can be apprehend with eyes and heart, the texts of this world that pull ideals down from the ether like, say, the books of Gandhi.

Father and son are opposites not just metaphysically but physically as well. Anjan Bacchu, the son, is a pudgy, baby-faced twenty-something who wears his profession, computer programming, on his sleeve—usually a nerdy outfit consisting of a golf shirt and Dockers-like slacks. His thick black hair is always slightly unkempt. He is a young man, younger in personality than his twenty-eight years, still clearly in search of his path in the world. Anjan's father, M.A. Bacchu, is thin-faced, almost gaunt, his dark brown eyes set deep inside his head under carefully combed salt-and-pepper hair. His voice, too, is thin, and his delivery a rapid, high-pitched rasp compared to Anjan's lyrical and plaintive speech.

Regard them as they stand side by side, and it is not immediately obvious that M.A. and Anjan are father and son. But look into their large, round, deep brown eyes. There is resemblance after all: In them, emotions are as obvious as wind rippling the surface of a limpid lake. There is resemblance also in the way they smile: the way their heads tilt back and slightly to one side, their teeth suddenly showing. There is nothing forced; theirs is true joy when they break out in laughter, which is often.

But what father and son have most in common is the world, as seen from their corner of the globe. Both were born and raised in Bangalore,

India, and live there in the midst of momentous and disturbing change: the complete restructuring of the economy, with the attendant cultural transformation. One of the fastest-growing cities in Asia, Bangalore is India's fifth largest, with a population of nearly six million. Capital of the state of Karnataka, it sits on a plateau in the temperate southern region of the country. A city at the heart of India's centuries of conquests, famines, colonialism, rebellion, arts, and spirituality, it has earned many nicknames: "The Garden City," "Pub City of India," Fruit Market of South India." In the last twenty years, it has earned yet another: "Silicon Valley of India." Bangalore is host to a galaxy of multinational tech companies, and in recent years its computer exports have expanded exponentially. It also exports programmers by the thousands to the Silicon Valley of California, under the aegis of the controversial H1-B Visa program. Hundreds of thousands of these visas were handed out to hi-tech workers during the boom of the 1990s, South Asians securing the majority of them. The program, like other guest-worker initiatives, was criticized by both nativist conservatives and labor-friendly liberals.

In the end, no matter how much they quarrel, Anjan Bacchu is Mr. M.A. Shetty Bacchu's son, and India is his father's house, the country that both men love and that Anjan must now leave: History has stepped into their lives in the form of one of those coveted visas.

::

From Anjan's point of view, the matter is simple: Why live and work in the Silicon Valley of India, working for a fraction of the salary he would receive in the Silicon Valley of California? The calculation is easy enough, and Anjan knows it by heart. It is a calculation made every day by prospective migrants throughout the developing world, whether they are hi-tech workers like Anjan, peasant families in Mexico, Dominicans with major-league baseball dreams, Ogonis on the Niger Delta or Palestinians on the West Bank. The political situations in these lands are strikingly different, as are the base economic conditions among those dreaming of a better life beyond the homeland, but all these migrants subjectively occupy the same position relative to what they believe they can achieve in America. It is the essence of their ambition.

But as with so many things in his life, Anjan is ambivalent about his career and the global economy it is utterly connected to. In Bangalore, Anjan works for an Indian company that contracts his services to Motorola-India. Anjan could make much more money by working directly for Motorola, but the prospect of working for a multinational company (MNC) in India would compromise his deep-rooted sense of Nehruvian nationalism. (Notwithstanding the financial sacrifice to maintain his posture, Anjan is making more at twenty-eight years of age than his father M.A. ever did.) But then Anjan announces his desire to work for a company in America. Anjan's beloved Nehru would surely have had some strong words for him. Yes, Anjan, you will surely find riches in that Valley of Silicon, but you will be denying India the best you have to offer!

It's called the "brain drain," the exodus of countless skilled employees.

Anjan would become one of the 240,000 Indians who left the motherland between 2000 and 2002, according to figures from the Center for Immigration Studies. (The International Council on Education estimates that nearly half of the country's newly graduated engineers and scientists go abroad for work, not just to the States, but also to the new technology centers of Canada, Australia, New Zealand, and across Europe). It is perhaps the greatest emigration in India's history.

::

It is a sign of the times in the Silicon Valley of India that Anjan Bacchu, computer programmer and bachelor, meets the woman he will marry through a computer-aided marriage bureau. (These proliferate in India today; log on to the *Times of India*, and the link for its matchmaking section is just below the banner.) Anjan chose a company, logged on, and answered the requisite questions, providing information about himself as well as what he sought in a "life partner." Singles are asked to provide information about caste, level of education, income, and even one's *nakshatra* (personality traits in the Hindu Vedic astrological system). The virtual matchmaker suggested a woman by the name of Harshini Radhakrishnan, a computer instructor from the nearby town of Mysore. In response to Anjan's initial entreaty, Harshini wrote that she was a "cool girl" looking for a "cool guy." Anjan has enough self-awareness to know that he's anything but, yet he was so smitten with Harshini's image on the computer screen—her long-faced beauty and round, open eyes—that he couldn't bring himself to reveal his techie nerdness in the early stages of the digi-romance. When the actual, corporeal meeting took place, Harshini's illusions of finding a hip husband were quickly dispelled; she met a guy whose glasses are constantly sliding down his nose. But there was something endearing about Anjan—his wide-eyed, boyish eagerness, his tenderness and vulnerability, and his material ambitions.

Technology may be changing the way India conducts its cultural business, but as for the essence of the culture, the change is subtle. In a country with a long tradition of arranged marriages, the computer has merely replaced human matchmakers; Anjan and Harshini dutifully accepted the choice of the digital gods.

Their meeting took place in late 1998, well before the bursting of the Silicon Valley bubble. Had it taken place after, Harshini might have said no; these days, un- or underemployed computer geeks are at the bottom of India's marriage pool.

Two weeks after their first physical meeting, Anjan traveled to Mysore to celebrate their engagement. On a bus filled with family and friends, including his best friend Vishwa (a huge teddy bear of a man), Anjan takes the typical ribbing in stride, standing in the aisle and hoisting a small red boom box playing Hindi songs sung by Harshini. But in his head, there's a constant dialogue going on. Is he really ready for marriage? His father has been pressuring him for some time to get serious about life. How serious can a twenty-eight year old be if he's still a childless bachelor? The other voice is that of his ambition. Just a few days ago, the American immigration authorities approved his petition for a visa, and Microsoft immediately offered him a programming job in California. The timing was bad. He'd just met and proposed to Harshini, and the preparation for the wedding would take plenty of time.

Decision time: Get married or dash off into a California future?

Decision time, indeed. And Anjan had put off such momentous life decisions for years. He lay awake nights, knots in his stomach, the pendulum swinging from head to heart, from heart to head: Harshini, Microsoft . . . Microsoft, Harshini.

He finally called Microsoft and said no. M.A. was happy—finally his son had listened! But some of Anjan's friends were stunned. Refuse a job from the undisputed giant of the global digital realm just to stay a few more months in India to get married? You're a fool, one said. You're nuts, said another. But Anjan had made peace with his ambivalence: Now, he would follow his heart—and later, his head. Life was about balancing both. Perhaps, Anjan thought, he could even broker a treaty between his father's world of spirit and Anjan's more earthly desires of career, money, and creature comforts. Maybe he could even make peace with his father.

Anjan at prayer

::

The engagement ceremony is held under a shamiana tent on Harshini's father's property. Dozens of members of each family sit at long tables. Anjan and Harshini are side by side, the young pair with the nervous smiles. Servants ladle great gobs of rice onto the guests' plates. The *puja*, as Hindi rituals of worship are called, invokes the gods of the Hindi cosmos, Ganesha, Varun Devta, Laxmi, and Narayan, Brahma, Vishnu, Shiva, and the gods of the nine planets of the solar system. The incense burns, the hollow hum of the harmonium and rapid finger-slapping of the tabla fill the air. At the climax of the ceremony, Anjan and Harshini stand in the center of the hall and hang bright garlands around each other's necks. The engagement is now sacred. Anjan and Harshini's destinies are joined, as are their families. But the destiny of the couple is also joined to the vicissitudes of the government and the economy of the United States of America. Their relationship to one another—how close they are or how far apart, in the spiritual and the spatial sense—will to a great degree depend on things like the NASDAQ and interest rates and immigration officers, on information and capital, on a desire that will be expressed in the zeroes and ones of computer code.

::

It's a few weeks before the wedding. Harshini and Anjan shop in downtown Bangalore. The sights and sounds on the street are a jumble of distinct worlds colliding: Barefoot women balance great baskets of produce on their heads outside in the shadow of a gleaming mall. The choking traffic on the avenues is a blend of centuries—bicycles and scooters and cows and paupers and neon and Mercedes—the few rich and the many, many poor of India.

I wonder if Anjan feels guilty about shopping . . . does he hear his father's voice as he walks past the armed guards into the mall?

"Some of the ideals that I have in my life came from my father," Anjan says. "It's he who told about Gandhi, Nehru, about truthfulness, purity. But then again, there are many things that because of our father-son relationship . . . we quarrel. These shoes I have were two thousand rupees. I go to restaurants sometimes, or a good food festival and spend fifteen hundred, two thousand, stuff like that, and he doesn't like it."

At home—Anjan the bachelor still lives at home, as is common pretty much everywhere in the world except America—M.A. is merciless when he lectures his son.

"I see you as a diamond," father says, "but somehow I failed to polish you. See the polishing, it's . . ." (Here, he pantomimes, as if he were grinding a huge black rock.) ". . . it might not be very nice for him to hear this, but if only I'd polished him better!"

Father is sitting on the floor—the spitting image of Gandhi—and son is towering over him as M.A. says all this with an incongruous smile on his face. But how small Anjan feels!

::

As beautiful and complex as the engagement ceremony is, it pales in comparison to the wedding, an epic ritual of incense and henna and toe rings and veils and dancing, dizzying intonations from the priest and effusive notes from the musicians. The Silicon Valley of California disappears in the flames of the holy fire into which the newlyweds sprinkle offerings of ghee, or clarified butter. Time disappears: We are in an India innocent of MTV, in the Eden of the precolonial, not in the throes of globalization. For a moment, time is nothing, place is everything, and Anjan and Harshini are at the center of the Hindu universe, young lovers in love.

::

And then time reappears.

Anjan, back to his practical, career-driven self, sets a timeline of two months for "adjustment" to the matrimonial life. All the while, he hunts for jobs in the Silicon Valley of California.

Anjan is a tough negotiator in his overseas conversations with prospective placement agencies. One demands a "bench clause," which allows the company to reduce wages to a pittance of a retainer should Anjan find himself out of work.

"But I have five years' experience," Anjan spits out. "I don't deserve a bench clause!"

M.A. shakes his head. "He so very choosy," he says. "If he does not get what he wants he may not go at all." Nevertheless—and uncharacteristically—father accepts responsibility for what he perceives to be the son's faults. "My characteristics have passed on to him. For some things sometimes, we will not compromise for anything!"

A week later, after blowing off the company demanding the bench clause, Anjan signs on with a smaller company . . . and accepts a bench clause.

Father shakes his head again. "He didn't get the job of his choice. Why he has compromised, I don't know."

::

How bewildering, how troubling it is for the older generation of India to look upon the brain-drain generation. Days before Anjan's departure to America, Anjan, M.A., and a few of his father's friends discuss the gap, the argument between the old and the new, between India and America, between the material world and the world of spirit.

M.A.: "Just go and get the money, I say that's nonsense."

Another elder (apologizing for Anjan): "Here [in India] because we are not able to get the money, we go to the other direction."

Yet another elder (invoking Nehru): "Let [Anjan] come back and be associated with his own nation."

First elder: "But once you get addicted to that type of living, probably you will not be able to come back because of the . . ."

A third elder: "The conveniences there."

First elder (to Anjan): "Don't go with the intention of settling there."

M.A. (increasingly passionate): "More than anything, it is a question of patriotism. He must come and serve India, that's first. You must be true to your mother first. No country has produced as intelligent people [as India]. No saints have come as much as from India, no scientists have come as much as we have produced in India. Yet we are also the poorest country . . . and we just give [our best] to America and Britain and France and Germany. All the rich cream they are taking!"

And now, they are taking his son.

::

In typical migrant tradition, Anjan will leave for America first, establish himself, save up some money, and only then send for Harshini. He got an earful of advice on the topic from his father and his father's friends—most of them urging him to take her along from the beginning, but he stuck to his original plan. Anjan likes plans. He's always composing lengthy to-do lists in his cramped, intricate handwriting.

If Harshini complains at all about being left behind, she does so in private. India, like most developing world societies, remains strictly patriarchal. Harshini dutifully cooks and cleans for her husband at home. And yet, I wonder whether she'll remain the tradition-bound wife once she joins Anjan in California. Globalization is having an impact on gender roles. I've seen Mexican migrant women in the U.S. drive cars and even tractors—virtually unimaginable in the Mexican provinces—and I've seen Mexican migrant men in the U.S. begin to share work around the house. It is a matter of acculturation to the mores of the migrants' new home, and it is a matter of the economy as well. Women who've never left the house and kids in the Old World suddenly enter the American workforce, giving them a sense of empowerment they'd never experienced. Many American-born women are still bitter about lingering sexism, but from a migrant woman's point of view, the new country offers utter liberation. The signs are all around them, in the neighborhoods, in their places of work and in pop culture. It is a situation that has caused many a macho a gender-based headache.

But Anjan and Harshini don't have to deal with that yet. They are barely embarking on their journey, at the very cusp of the changes it will surely bring.

::

As his departure date approaches, Anjan's level of anxiety increases, so much so that he goes to the doctor for a checkup. His "bad" cholesterol must come down, the doc says, adding that the stress of the impending trip is probably weighing heavy on his body as well. And, of course, he just got married. And he's going to be starting a new job. Dealing with a new culture.

But there are other "inputs," Anjan confides to Harshini, using digital lingo. What he finds himself thinking about, worrying about the most these days is his father. His health is deteriorating. He has cirrhosis of the liver and diabetes.

Like so many tense father-son relationships, it appears that M.A. and Anjan have little way of expressing their love for one another if not through emotional or intellectual violence. The long-running argument continues.

"I'm sorry to say that I have a very low estimation of the American people," M.A. says to Anjan a few days before he leaves. "I feel sorry for them. With power, with money, they are still poor people; they are very, very poor."

Anjan must defend the ideals of the country that he is emigrating to. "America as a country is all about the individual. Freedom of the individual."

M.A., of course, is not swayed. "They do not know what is freedom. Freedom from what? Freedom from ambition? Freedom from anger? Freedom from vices? From what they are free? Tell me one thing in which they are free?"

"Freedom of speech," Anjan retorts.

"Freedom of speech for what?" M.A. comes back immediately. His arms are folded over his chest, the stern lecturer. "Do you think I get something because I have all the freedom to talk? And these politicians talk so much, do you think it is worth something? No. Freedom to talk when it is responsible to talk, not when you are just talking because you know how to talk. What the great teachers have said is that their words turn to pearls when they speak."

M.A. utters this last sentence in Kannada, his maternal tongue (and the state language of Karnataka), as if to lay the trump card on the conversation by code-switching to the tongue of the wise ancients and putting the crude, upstart Americans in their place.

Long-running argument between father and son, round 11: Anjan, backed into a corner, is left speechless.

::

Harshini and Anjan celebrate their first wedding anniversary days shy of his departure for the States. They visit a temple for prayer and meditation. An emaciated dog stands at the entrance to the old limestone building. The monks chant, the incense burns. Afterward, the couple sits silently by the edge of a reflecting pool, their inverted images wavering on the brownish water.

Anjan is pensive. A year ago he was a bachelor who knew the language of C+ and C++ better than the language of love. A year ago, all that seemed to matter was leaving the Silicon Valley of India for the real Silicon Valley. Initially, he even thought of marriage as less of a spiritual matter than a practical one—he'd heard that he would have a better chance at landing an American work visa if he married. No matter how hard Anjan tries to break free of tradition, history always seems to reel him back in, and history speaks with his father's voice.

"There's a conflict in me," Anjan says. "The ideal, and the base personalities. I like worldly things. But I would also like to know what life is all about, what Buddha was seeking."

And now his father's voice rings in his ears. "I'm sure there'll be temples over there, but can we get peace over there? The vibration you get in a temple here might not be available over there. But then again, peace is here [he points to his head]."

On the morning of his departure, the Bacchu house in Bangalore is like a sepulchre. Anjan finishes packing. The huge suitcases are on the verge of bursting open. Harshini cries quietly in another room. Everyone dresses up for the occasion. A journey from the Old World to the New is just as momentous as a wedding, first communion, or a funeral.

The farewell at the airport is wrenching. Anjan makes a game attempt to maintain his composure as he says good-bye to Harshini, but the tears come.

"God is there, Anjan," Harshini tells him. She means that God is in America, too.

Anjan admonishes her to check her Yahoo! account regularly for his E-mails.

Now it is time to say good-bye to his best friend, Vishwa. The gentle giant urges him on. "Try your level best to settle down fast. I'll send you some E-mail and tell you everything. And I'll take care of him," Vishwa says, referring to Anjan's ailing father. This comment brings a fresh burst of tears from Anjan. He cries like a lost child, burying his head in Vishwa's huge chest.

The final farewell is between father and son. M.A. kisses him on both cheeks, and then on his forehead. Then a long embrace, Anjan laying his head over his father's bony shoulder. Anjan closes his eyes. He looks like a slumbering baby.

::

Anjan watches the plane's slow but inexorable eastward trajectory over the Pacific Ocean on a monitor at the head of the economy cabin. He's hard at work on a new to-do list. The tears are gone.

But even the most detailed to-do list cannot prepare you for life's cruelest blows. One month after arriving in America, Anjan will receive the news that his best friend Vishwa is dead, killed in a motor scooter accident. There will be no way for Anjan to breach the 9,000 miles separating him from his homeland, and his best friend's ashes.

::

When my mother departed El Salvador for the States in 1957 at the age of twenty, her image of America came mostly from old copies of *Good Housekeeping* that had made their way back to the Old Country with relatives returning home for the occasional visit. It was a land where women could wear pants (even blue jeans!), a place where everyone was born with a birthright to the middle class, to huge platters of meat on the dinner table every night. These were the images that Vilma Angulo (my mother's maiden name) held in her mind when she boarded a Pan

American bimotor for the then quite lengthy flight to San Francisco. Her arrival bolstered the visions. The plane banked over the bay at dawn, offering a view of the windows of downtown office buildings and Victorian houses on the hills glinting with the break of day. Later, she would see poverty and race riots and protests against the war in Vietnam, but San Francisco in 1957, especially in comparison to the tattered homeland she left behind, did indeed look to my mother like the mythic shining city on a hill.

Such auspicious arrivals are more rare for immigrants these days. For one thing, the signs of America have proliferated the world over; there's a McDonald's in every capital on the globe, a glut of American products visible on the streets and on cinema or TV or computer screens. For many migrants, this translates into less of an initial sense of dislocation in that they are arriving in a territory whose landscape has been etched on their minds practically since birth. But while the signs may be familiar, the context, of course, is not. It's one thing to experience McDonald's in the developing world (in Mexico, jalapeño salsa accompanies the Big Mac); it is quite another for a Mexican to order a taco at Taco Bell.

Nation-states may be crumbling in theory and free trade zones accelerating the process of global integration in practice, but to cross a border, to ford a river or wall, or fly over an ocean en route to a new land is still a bewildering experience.

::

Anjan Bacchu arrives at San Francisco airport on a gray rainy day—nary a ray of sunlight to make the city gleam. In any case, his destination is not San Francisco, with its splendid mix of architectures rising from hill and dale, but the horizontal vistas of San Jose, Santa Clara, Milpitas, Sunnyvale: the suburban flatlands south of the city that are known as Silicon

In Silicon Valley

Valley. On the northern end of California's Great Central Valley, the region was largely agricultural until the mid-twentieth century, when first semiconductor and later microchip development and manufacturing firms expanded outward from the main research node at Stanford University in Palo Alto. Most of the technology that we use today in personal and business computing was initially conceived by Cold War geeks in the region. By the 1970s, postindustrial parks began to emerge—sprawling tech centers known as "campuses," collections of block-long megaliths with few windows and typically surrounded by a touch of green space (perfectly trimmed lawn grass that looked more like Astroturf) and bordered by tall iron fences. The ultimate visual effect was distinctly inhuman, as if the tech industry was a thing unto itself, needing no living custody. But, of course, legions of human workers were needed. As the industry grew, the peculiar Silicon Valley landscape emerged. Beyond the old city centers with their venerable Deco office buildings and Victorian and Craftsman homes, the orchards were transformed into swathes of cheaply built one- or two-story apartment complexes to house the techies. Today, there is a severe housing shortage in the area, due to little or ill-conceived planning and Northern California geography.

"I'm looking for tall buildings, and this is what I see," Anjan grumbles, peering past the rain-speckled windshield of the car driven by Mr. Shubankar, a fellow countryman who works at Impetus Computing Systems, the firm that will contract Anjan's services out into the galaxy of companies in the region.

Shubankar advises Anjan to hit the ground running. Within a couple of hours of his arrival, he deposits Anjan at the company's credit union, where he has the first of many encounters with what an Indian might call the caste system of America. A Vietnamese intake worker asks Anjan to fill out a form that asks the primordial question of race.

Anjan puzzles over the form.

"I'm not white," he says mostly to himself, and the intake worker giggles. "And I'm not Hispanic. I'm not Black. I guess . . ."

"Just check the one that's closest," the intake worker advises.

Anjan Bacchu checks the box next to "Asian."

Later, Anjan sits down at a nearby restaurant for his first full, public meal in America. His waiter is another immigrant, apparently from the Middle East. They both speak in English with their distinct accents. They can barely understand one another. Anjan is a vegetarian and intent on remaining one in the meat-crazed West, so he studies the menu carefully.

What is calamari? Anjan asks. It's a kind of seafood, the waiter replies.

Is it vegetarian? Anjan inquires. No, responds the waiter.

Anjan cuts to the chase: What do you have here that is vegetarian?

The waiter suggests artichoke, which Anjan has never heard of. Anjan presses further. Does the waiter understand that vegetarian means no egg also? No egg, no fish in an artichoke?

The waiter advises that artichoke (which he describes as a "fruit") indeed would be the best vegetarian choice at the restaurant, which is a typical American diner.

So now Anjan needs to know what is this thing called an artichoke.

Imagine the Middle Eastern waiter trying to explain to the newly arrived Indian immigrant what an artichoke is.

Anjan decides to risk it and orders the artichoke and a bowl of vegetable soup. When the soup arrives, he eyes it carefully. Strange concoction. He is unaware that there may well be chicken or beef broth in it. He tries a spoonful. The taste is utterly foreign. So . . . *bland.*

The artichoke arrives, on a plate garnished with slices of tomato and leaves of iceberg lettuce. What is to be done with this bizarre fruit? The waiter said something about the leaves. Anjan picks one and puts the entire thing in his mouth. A few bites and he spits it out. Pushes the artichoke plate aside. Back to the soup; he reaches for the saltshaker, and he shakes and shakes and shakes it. He tries the soup again. He nods his head. Now that's better.

::

Anjan decides to shop for the essentials with checklist (in a spiral notebook) in hand. At a convenience store, he looks for a map and an umbrella, and has a tough time of it communicating with the Chinese clerks. Indian staples are next on the list, but where does one buy saffron here? Luckily, he runs into a couple of countrymen as he ambles aimlessly down the street. They speak Kannada, they are from Anjan's home state, and they point him in the direction of an Indian store. He buys saffron and a stainless steel serving plate, an omnipresent utensil in Indian cooking. And the one item no immigrant the world over can do without: a phone card.

Home is a corner of a small bedroom in the typical Silicon Valley housing complex. Several Indian programmers, all bachelors, share the apartment; most of the units are used the same way. At the height of the tech boom, overblown salaries combined with a housing shortage to send rents skyrocketing—one- or two-bedroom apartments ran as high as $2,500 per month. And it is not as if these are fancy buildings with doormen and housecleaning included with the rent. They are the typical wood-shingled exterior, dry-walled interior models, most of them built in the last few decades. In fact, there is little to distinguish these complexes from those that house Mexican and Asian immigrants not far away in the "inner-city" sections of San Jose, except the fact that in those, five or six men may sleep in a single bedroom (with another several on the living-room floor), and none of them have jobs with hi-tech salaries and benefits. But the same principle of migrant economic solidarity is at work in these disparate settings. There is no way a single Indian tech worker or a single Mexican landscaper would throw money at an apartment for the sake of "privacy." The migrant goal, after all, is to save money in the present to prepare the future for nuclear and even extended family in America. And so the migrant solidarity network does what it does best: maximizes production and minimizes cost.

The walls of the apartment are bare, not a single photograph, poster, or tapestry to offset the uniform beige walls. The place is not exactly tidy, but neither is it especially clean. There's a brood of single men living here, after all—Old World men getting a first taste of picking up after themselves, washing clothes, and cooking meals.

Shortly after arriving at the apartment, Anjan picks up the phone to dial home. The virtual operator guides him through the various operations to make the connection. He must dial the calling card number and then his PIN number and then the number for long distance access and then the country code and then the city code and finally Harshini's number, at which point the operator says, "Your current balance will allow you to talk for thirty-six minutes."

Busy signal.

Anjan goes through the digits again.

Busy signal.

And again.

Busy signal.

And again.

Busy signal.

He never does reach home on his first day in America.

::

The first few weeks of Anjan's new life in America go relatively smoothly. Impetus succeeds in placing him with 2Wire, a startup firm developing "intelligent home appliances." The offices of the company are styled like much else in Silicon Valley: minimally. There is a logo outside the building, of course, but inside the walls are as bare as Anjan's apartment. Capital is moving so rapidly in the region that the global tech circus seems to want to be ready to pull up stakes at a moment's notice. The moment will come soon enough.

By day, Anjan sits in his cubicle and pounds out code, and he studies code at night in the apartment. The practical side of Anjan has taken over, and he realizes it. He might as well be inside the walls of a tech firm

At work

in Bangalore, for all that he's seen of America. He's trapped in the hi-tech ghetto, alongside tens of thousands of his countrymen. "It's not like I'm really living in the U.S.," he says ruefully. "I wanted to see the world. It's not that I am disappointed just knowing Indians, but I guess at the same time I also wanted to get exposed to more people."

Is Anjan typical of New Americans these days? And are these new Americans any different than the immigrants of old? The argument over assimilation goes back decades, and it is being vetted again in the global era. For all the arguments Americans make in favor of assimilation—leave your past behind at the gates to America, join the melting pot—the American economy works against it by dividing labor into ethnic enclaves as much as ethnics seek to establish them for essential first-gen-eration solidarity. South Asians are merely the latest in a long line of immigrants herded into labor-thirsty niches. Before them came the Mexicans who worked the fields, and the Poles in meatpacking and the Portuguese fishermen. Just as there are economic niches, so too there are housing niches; Americans may complain that the immigrants "stick together" too much, but historically segregation has played its part as well. Little Mexico and Little Italy and Little India are as much a measure of "our" distrust of "them" as they are of the first generation's need to recreate a semblance of the Old World in the New.

To assimilate or not to assimilate? The scale of today's wave of immigration rivals that of the early twentieth-century infusion, fanning fears of "Balkanization." But it is not so much a matter of the numbers involved as it is how technology has transformed the way we communicate. Today's migrants make contact with the Old World much more easily than their forebears. Not only do they phone home (when the lines aren't busy) and talk to loved ones, they can use the Internet to E-mail home and virtually visit, or get a satellite-TV hookup and tune in Al Jazeera or Doordarshan, one of India's national networks.

::

Had my mother emigrated as a young Salvadoran woman today and I were born into the global realm, would my cultural personality be different, and how? Would I speak more Spanish, less English, be a better Catholic, still live with my parents? My guess is that the specter of cultural separatism is both overblown by our own neoimperial projections (the "War on Terror") and a sign of real change. Regionalism and cultural nationalism—occasionally fanatical—seems to rise in direct response to the economic push toward "one world" precisely because globalization, seen from the perspective of the developing countries and the legions of their emigrants in the West, seems to offer riches mostly to those who are white, male, speak English, and uphold unfettered capitalism as the essential pillar of democracy. But assimilation was never a scientific model to begin with. At what point is an immigrant considered assimilated? When one changes one's name from, say, Emmanuel Rudnitsky to Man Ray? My father argues that my Mexican grandparents were assimilated in spite of the fact they never learned to speak English well because they opened a savings account, bought a house, and paid their taxes in America (assimilation as more of an economic fact than a cultural one). Most social scientists today refer to the process of change that occurs when one comes to a new country as acculturation—an adaptation, not a whole-scale transformation. The acculturated migrant is somewhere in between Old and New worlds, in between languages, mores, and tastes in music and clothes and food. The in-between space is dynamic and ever shifting.

It is the space that Anjan occupies in America, one he began to occupy even before he arrived. These days, you don't have to leave the East to be influenced by the West; the West arrived in Bangalore in the form of the microchip, materialism, and American pop. One day, Anjan frets that his long work hours at 2Wire don't allow him enough time to perform his yoga rituals; the next, he will excitedly chatter about his knowledge of Enterprise Java Beans technology and his increased dollar value in the IT market as a result (Impetus makes $20,000 a month by contracting his services to 2Wire; Anjan gets $5,000 of it).

It appears that there's no way out of the ambivalent space. Given the reach of the global, Anjan would still be in-between even if he'd never left India.

::

Anjan is back at San Francisco International, but he is neither arriving nor departing this time. Harshini is finally joining him in America.

As soon as he sees her exiting Customs, Anjan scampers toward her with boyish excitement. Harshini asks him why he hasn't cut his hair. It's as unruly as ever. Anjan swears to cut it the next day. They embrace and sway as if dancing to a slow beat.

"Show me the house quickly, won't you?" Harshini says.

Anjan has finally left the Impetus guesthouse and its messy bachelor life behind, renting a one-bedroom apartment in a classic Silicon Valley complex, his first step in American upward mobility. Harshini takes off her shoes and touches the ground before entering and getting the grand tour from Anjan. Here's the kitchen with the electric stove and many, many cupboards. And here's the hallway, and the bedroom . . . the walls are brilliant white and bare, as is most of the apartment (there will be much shopping). And here is the surprise: a walk-in wardrobe closet for Harshini! Back in the kitchen, she asks Anjan where he bought the plates and how much they cost. Anjan says that they were $7.50. For just one? That's 350 rupees, Anjan says. They will be talking about such things a lot in the coming months.

::

They sit in the living room, on bland IKEA-looking sofa and chair. Anjan is talking about Vishwa, his best friend, now dead. Remember at the airport in Bangalore? He told Anjan that it would only be a matter of a couple of years before Anjan returned to India, that in the meantime Vishwa would take care of M.A. And he told Anjan that he'd call him when Harshini arrived in America. Everything will be fine; it's only a matter of time, a short time.

And in a short time, Vishwa was dead.

Anjan cries softly.

"Don't keep talking about it," Harshini says. "I'll get depressed."

"I'm done," says Anjan.

::

Time goes on, a collection of moments.

Harshini, in stylish sunglasses, at the wheel of a smart new sport coupe at a car dealership (she settles for a used Toyota Camry).

Anjan and Harshini on their first vacation, a weekend at Lake Tahoe, Harshini's first sight of snow and her first snowball.

Shopping for clothes and gadgets at the mall. At San Francisco International, Anjan and Harshini joyfully receive Harshini's parents.

Anjan reads the *San Francisco Examiner*: Intel and Cisco Systems lay off thousands of employees.

Anjan in line at a job fair; he's been laid off at 2Wire.

Anjan and Harshini snap at each other about the price of a winter coat at the mall.

They pack up a U-Haul truck, its side panel emblazoned with the Statue of Liberty, and move into a smaller apartment.

And then, 9/11.

::

The waters of the Hudson are dark and gray as the sky over Manhattan.

"I hope you will join me now," says the Ellis Island tour guide, "in some silence so that we can pay our respects to the thousands of victims . . ."

The trip to New York is one last fling for the couple before Harshini returns to India. Anjan has bounced from one job to another; his

KARTEMQUIN FILMS

prospects for employment are about as certain as betting on the NAS-DAQ. Without a job, his status in the U.S. becomes vulnerable; by the letter of the immigration law, if he is unemployed, he is considered "out of status" on his H1-B visa and subject to eventual deportation.

Bundled up and smacking his gloved hands together, Anjan finally sees the tall buildings he always associated with America.

"The Empire State Building," the tour guide calls out. "Once again, the tallest building in New York City."

The farewell at SFO will be as hard for Anjan as when he said goodbye to Harshini, his father, and Vishwa in Bangalore two years ago. The migrant life is an emotional roller coaster, an endless series of arrivals and departures, dictated by invisible forces that have such a visible, visceral impact on our lives.

"Give me your tired, your poor, your huddled masses yearning to breathe free . . ." intones the tour guide.

He will find a job. He will work hard. He will do yoga at four in the morning and leave for work by six and be the first to arrive. He will buy phone cards and call home and coo to his baby daughter 9,000 miles away.

"... the wretched refuse of your teeming shore ..."

Or maybe, jobless, he will return home. Or maybe, if the economy turns up again, he will bring Harshini and his baby back to America.

"... Send these, the homeless, tempest-tossed to me ..."

He will be alone in America, alone as any immigrant in America.

"I lite my lamp beside the golden door."

Liberty raises her torch into the freezing rain.

The Narrative of Exile :: Mira Nair

In late December of 2001, I traveled to Guatemala City for a cousin's wedding. It was the first time in well over a decade that most of my mother's extended family had gotten together, and we were aware that it would probably be the last reunion of its kind. In another ten years, my mother's mother will be dead and my mother's own generation will reach that age when people say things like, "Every day that God grants me now is a gift," precisely what my maternal grandfather said in his seventies, as he battled the lung cancer to which he eventually succumbed.

My family had been scattered by the same winds that move the world today: politics, economy, individual will. My mother, née Vilma Angulo, was the first of her generation to leave Central America, emigrating at the age of twenty, arriving first in San Francisco and later Los Angeles, where she met my father, and I was born. But the migrations in my family actually began much earlier. An iconoclastic aunt of my mother's claimed the title of clan pioneer in the States, arriving in Los Angeles in the 1930s. A black-sheep uncle roamed the north for years – California, New York, Canada. Another uncle settled in Miami and one of his children wound up in Houston, Texas, where I now have a brood of distant cousins.

I could go further back. My great-grandfather, my mother's paternal grandfather, was born in Jalisco, Mexico, and sought his fortune in Central America in the late nineteenth century; his father had emigrated from Spain. All in all, over the past century and a half, my mother's extended family has migrated as far north as Canada and as far south as Chile. As a result, my family is exceedingly mixed in ethnic terms. We are light-skinned and dark, our noses are thick, flared, and Mayan, and Spanish-thin, our hair kinky and straight. We are lovers of the Other.

Soon after I was born, my uncle and aunt arrived in the States, lured mostly, I believe, by the currents of American pop. They listened to Sonny and Cher and watched Apollo rockets thundering into the sky on a black-and-white TV set in a living room from within the borders of modernity itself — not thousands of miles away in the tropics, where one always seemed to receive Western style and news a day late and badly dubbed. Both ultimately returned to El Salvador after learning of modernity's discontents (race riots, inflation, life as work), but their children retraced their footsteps to the U.S., and made movement a constant in their own lives. Some cousins arrived in Los Angeles, others settled in Hawaii and in northern California; today, I even have family in Denver, Colorado. Me, I've lived in Los Angeles, San Salvador, Mexico City, Guatemala City, the Mojave Desert, Boston, and Houston.

My cousin Sonia's wedding took place in Guatemala because that is where much of my Salvadoran family has lived for the past decade. My aunt and uncle, Sonia's parents, had moved from San Salvador to Guatemala City in the early 1990s; my uncle was lucky enough to find a job in textile management and whisk the family out of the ceaseless anxiety of civil war. (Of course, their new country itself was still in the throes of its own conflict — one even bloodier than El Salvador's — but the violence there was largely contained to the rural and Indian north.) They bought a home in a new middle-class subdivision on the outskirts of the capital. They own two cars, have a live-in maid, and shop at a classic American-style mall just up the road.

My uncle Ramón is a devout and conservative Catholic (a follower, in fact, of the Opus Dei order, which played an important behind-the-scenes role supporting Salvador's status quo against Marxist rebels during the war). Ramón is a pure-blooded Spaniard, and that entire side of my family — light-skinned, thin-nosed, the elders still speaking Spanish with a Castilian accent — is very proud of that fact. Guests at their house are received with sangria and paella, as if they were a contemporary clan of conquistadors or missionaries only temporarily living among the heathens in the wild lands. His daughter's courtship was conducted Old World-strict. If there was any sex before marriage, it was and will be kept secret unto eternity.

My cousin would continue the family tradition by also marrying into a mixed family. Her fiancé was born in Guatemala City to a Guatemalan woman who'd married a barrel-chested American with crew-cut hair and a graduate degree in education (he established a private school in Guatemala).

My family from the States made the trip to Guatemala for the wedding – yet another mixed clan to add to the already blurry palette: my Mexican-American father, my Salvadoran mother and their three American-born kids, the gringo-est of all among the extended family. We arrived at my aunt's house a few days before the wedding, quickly filling up the last of the private spaces in the ample house. Soon there were relatives sleeping on all available furniture, and finally on the floor.

A motley crew indeed. A young cousin, a budding musician, quizzed me on the latest alt-rock acts in the States. An elder aunt reminded me, as she has for thirty years, that I am and will always be a Salvadoran first and foremost, for my mother was born on that sacred, beautiful patch of tropical earth. We spoke in English and Spanish and Spanglish. We ate wonderful, greasy Central American tamales one night and Kentucky Fried Chicken (up the street by the mall) the next. I was embarrassed by my Salvadoran family's earnest, cheesy efforts at Americanization as much as by their Old World ways, their provinciality, their claustrophobic family relations. And at the same time, I felt proud of both these tendencies.

The wedding reception was held, as is typical for the middle class in Latin America, at a country club. We danced to merengue and cumbia and oldies rock 'n' roll. My mother, the Old World girl who's spent forty-plus years in the States, cut loose, drinking, smoking, and tearing up the dance floor. We followed the Western marriage rituals right down to the bouquet of flowers and the garter thrown by bride and groom, respectively. And yet, I had the feeling that the ceremony was somehow all dressed up in drag. I've been to both classic American weddings and witnessed vows in the Indian highlands of Mexico, and this one seemed to lean toward the pagan.

And so when the bouquet hit my still-single-in-her-thirties sister in the head and she let it fall to the floor (there was no way she was going to catch it), and the garter hit me, the first-born son still-single-in-his-forties, squarely in the chest (despite my efforts to hide behind younger cousins), there was the sense that we'd been chosen not by North or South or East or West but by a force that transcended geographic notions of culture and history.

Family, like history, chooses you, and not the other way around. I felt suffocated and liberated. I am all of these things, I mused. I am all these things this effusive, confused brood is and more.

::

When I see *Monsoon Wedding*, Punjabi filmmaker Mira Nair's ode to her own middle-class family and its global ironies, a tremendous nostalgia comes over me. I screened the film in that bastion of middle-class intellectualism, Cambridge, Massachusetts. (At the time, I was at Harvard on a fellowship.) It was late winter of 2002, and my parents happened to be visiting at the time – their kid, a college dropout, had finally made it to the Ivy League, albeit on the cusp of middle age. We sat in a Kendall Square cineplex amid a mostly white audience, which laughed at the obvious – shall we say universal? – comedic material and sniffled through the pathos. But there were times when my parents and I were the only ones laughing or sniffling. The setting may have been Delhi, the code-switching between Hindi and English and Punjabi, the clothes a melding of saris and fat American pump heels, but it was my world projected onto the screen, the world of my transnational family. I felt boyishly giddy sitting there in the dark, laughing the laughter of recognition with my migrant mother and father – finally, we were on the silver screen!

Hollywood may have begun earnestly examining race in the 1960s – with movies like *Guess Who's Coming to Dinner, The Pawnbroker,* and others like them – but all these years later, people of color continue to have their place in American film: as the "help," as the terrorist, as the lusty señorita, as the gang-banger or the cartel kingpin. An interracial kiss is still rare enough to make news. Where is the image of our increasingly "mixed" America? Of "blaxican" children (the progeny of African Americans and Mexicans), the hip-hop Hmong, the Muslim Central Americans? It takes a Spike Lee to bring Italian, African American, Puerto Rican, and Asian characters together (*Do the Right Thing, Summer of Sam*), or a John Sayles to bring the U.S.-Mexico border's historical and cultural complexities to life (*Lone Star*). And it takes a Mira Nair to bring to life the idiosyncratic, kitschy, pathetic, heroic efforts of the transnational middle class to make sense of a world where space and time and the body are ever more manipulated by technology and the dot.com reality.

Nair's work on the transcultural – which began with Denzel Washington and Sarita Choudhury playing a young African American–Indian couple in 1991's *Mississippi Masala* – is unique on several fronts. Nair is a woman from a patri-archal Old World society who deftly explores issues of gender, sexual orienta-tion, class, and race. She is an Easterner who for years has lived in the West (she teaches film at Columbia University). And with *Monsoon Wedding,* she chose to frame her narrative in a predominately middle-class mise-en-scène. Within the rarefied world of artists who elect to explore the schisms and per-forations between cultures, it is even rarer to find one who begins the search from within her own social class.

Dissertations and documentaries about transnationalism almost invariably invoke the "marginal" subject – the workers of the world tossed this way and that by the winds of the global. Unquestionably, a humanist tendency is at the heart of this endeavor: The learned liberals would like to create awareness about the working classes of the world. And yet the most obvious of contradictions inherent in this project is rarely discussed: the class distance between observer and observed. It is not that postmodern academe is unaware of the problem – the academic term "reflexivity," which calls upon the observers to observe themselves and thus compensate for hidden preconceptions and prejudices, is a cornerstone of postmodern theory. What by and large has not changed is the observer's selection of subjects.

Given the continuing preponderance of Third World research subjects in the field, one would think that a prerequisite for transcultural status is to belong to the working classes. In the end, the typical subject today isn't much different than it was back in the days when anthropologists sought out "primitives," as if these could proffer a missing cultural and historical link between the modern and the premodern. Today's typical transnational documentary subject is the Third World denizen that comes into some form of contact with the First World: the aboriginal rapper, the code-switching bushman, the Indian who identifies with Britney Spears or Vin Diesel.

I myself am a practitioner of this questionable craft. I spent five years following an impoverished Mexican clan in their travels back and forth over the U.S.-Mexico border, and found myself scribbling notes about their taste for American basketball teams, hip-hop, and Chicken McNuggets. I'd grown up on the northern side of the border, understood these signs as my cultural lineage, and was fascinated – and that is the exact term – when my southern subjects suddenly took them as their own. The image of a Mexican peasant cheering on Michael Jordan is fascinating because of its sheer disjunctiveness. I undertook the ethnographer's typical reflexive path – tried to create a dialogue of subjectivities via "saturation reporting" and took care to disclose my own class origins – but to this day, I have nagging doubts as to how I ultimately portrayed my subjects. Did I really create a closer encounter, or merely reaffirm the distance between "us" and "them"?

(Underlying this problem is the postmodern conundrum of "the real," and for whom, and by whose power, and even whether, it exists. We live in an era obssessed with "reality television," with a mass audience that can be convinced of a social event's relevance and "authenticity" only through mass-media representation. But where is CNN's "reflexivity," with its reporters "embedded" on the killing fields of Iraq, or, for that matter, trapped in the self-censoring apparatus of beltway media?)

As a sociology student, Nair must have read all the latest postcolonial and feminist critiques of the canon, and done so from the position of having been born the subject of those very critiques. With *Monsoon Wedding*, she appears to suggest that the path toward a more honest representation is to foreground one's experience, one's place in the world, and draw in the Other through its lens.

Nair was a documentary filmmaker early in her career. She said that she grew tired of the form because she often found herself "waiting around for something to happen." In feature filmmaking, of course, that moment is born out of a collaboration between director, screenwriter, cinematographer, actors, art director, editor, composer, and a technical cast of thousands. Yet Nair's feature work retains a documentary feel, and not just because she often utilizes vérité style (*Monsoon* was shot in Super 16, with plenty of handheld camera work). Nair says that she wanted, above all else, to create an ode to the world she herself grew up in, the culturally vertiginous environment of the Delhi upper castes at the dawn of the global era. To be as "true" as possible to that world, she not only sought professional actors familiar with the territory but also invoked nontraditional casting. Several parts are played by Nair's own family members, including Nair's adolescent nephew Ishaan Nair, in the fairly prominent role of Varun Verma, the effeminate son of Lalit, the film's patriarch.

Monsoon's narrative takes us on a whirlwind tour of a Punjabi wedding in Delhi skewed by the currents of globalization. Aditi Verma, daughter of Lalit and Pimmi Verma, is to be wedded to Hemant Rai, a marriage arranged via long-distance telephone and Email between Delhi, where the Lalits live, and Houston, Texas, where Hemant lives and works. (Hemant's profession is never discussed, but we can take a guess that it has something to do with technology – he is clearly part of India's "brain drain" generation).

Sabrina Dhawan's script threads these disparate lives together in a Bollywoodesque soap of epic proportions, including lip-synched dance numbers and dark family secrets that power the narrative toward catharsis.

Several intimate relationships – all troubled, some abusive – swirl around the wedding couple. Lalit and Pimmi Verma, parents of the bride, are the elders trying to hold the family together against the winds of the global with the only power they know: tradition and ritual, which includes the groom riding in full regalia on a white horse, a huge wedding tent festooned with hundreds of marigold flowers, and plenty of Scotch whiskey.

Then there is cousin Rahul Chadha, who grew up in Australia and speaks with a decidedly Down Under accent. He falls for another Verma cousin, Ayesha, a "good Indian girl," and thus the perfect counterpoint to Rahul's foreign hipness that oozes liberal sexuality.

And there is the Vermas' domestic worker, a young Christian beauty surrounded by Hindus, who is wooed by P. K. Dubey, the wedding coordinator, a working-class guy beginning to taste a bit of upward mobility – and digital technology (he's got a cell phone, a pager, and a wristwatch that doubles as calculator).

Everyone has come together in honor of Aditi and Hemant, but even before the vows are exchanged, the relationship is on the rocks. It is a "semi-arranged" marriage – the young ones actually had some say in the matter – but still they are mostly strangers to one another, and they both chafe against the Old World custom. Especially Aditi, who has a lover in Delhi – a married TV talk-show host who revels in high-brow discussions about the "New India" – whom she finds hard to let go of even as Hemant arrives from Houston for the ceremony.

Between and among these relations there are three languages (English, Hindi, Punjabi), four continents (North America, Australia, the Indian subcontinent, and, of course, Europe), two religions (Hinduism, Christianity), and plenty of time (the jump-cutting of the MTV-present, India's millenary present-past). The musical soundtrack captures these disparate influences beautifully, with young Indian songwriters like Sukhwinder Singh, who contributed *"Aja Mera Jee Kardaa"* ("Today My Heart Desires"), a haunting composition drawing upon ancient Indian couplets performed in a kind of Punjabi-techno-rock style. (Mychael Danna composed the compelling and equally hybridized original score – the effusive polyphony of Indian strings, winds and electronica seem to rise from the very soot of Delhi's dizzyingly diverse streets – a stunning effort at transcultural aesthetics considering he grew up in a suburb of Winnipeg, Canada.)

Monsoon is not Bollywood-simple, nor is it a facile multicultural fable. The schisms between generations, mores, genders, East and West, produce a tension that explodes into emotional violence throughout the film. Transnational living can be sexy, Nair seems to be saying, and it is also terribly, frighteningly, unsettling. All the characters are looking for a semblance of home – temporal continuity, emotional rootedness, physical permanence – but the very idea of home is being steadily undone by a world order that is bulldozing the very idea of stability. The plot point upon which the film ultimately turns – the family nearly torn asunder by sexual abuse – seems to imply the metaphor of globalization itself as violation of what is most sacred about culture, the way it provides history and a sense of place in the world.

In the end, the family weathers the storm, literally and metaphorically. The wedding tent built by P.K. Dubey and his crew is torn apart by the deluge in the middle of the wedding ceremony, but the rain that envelops all – the abusers and abused, the elders and their rebellious progeny, the natives and those who live abroad – reminds us of what remains sacred even now, especially now: the relations of family and community, the only way to recreate "home" in our increasingly homeless lives.

Maybe the deluge had to fall for us to reaffirm ourselves.

The monsoon rain blesses Aditi and Hemant (she leaves behind the smarmy married talk-show host after all, and her groom rises to the occasion by offering her a second chance). It honors the sacrifice of Lalit and Pimmi, making of their efforts to rein in foreign influence among the clan less a quixotic venture than a necessary, countervailing force. It assuages the pain of Ria's and Aliya's abuse (and judges their abuser). It blends with P.K. Dubey's and Alice's tears of joy as they exchange their working class vows alongside Aditi and Hemant.

I walked out of the theater with my parents on a clear, warm New England day only a few months after our own family's version of *Monsoon Wedding*, and I vowed that I would do all I could to hold the ties that bind us together, no matter how far the winds blow us apart.

::

In the political lexicon of migration, human movement is defined schematically: One is a refugee or a political asylum-seeker, a legal or illegal immigrant. One moves for economic reasons, or political. (If you are of the upper castes and your name is known for political or literary reasons – if you wrote a poem, say, that insulted the dictator – you earn the title of exile, a kind of five-star émigré.)

These are neat little divisions that ignore the complexity of human desire and necessity. When there is a revolution or a monetary devaluation or earthquake or civil war in a country, in most cases a vast majority of the citizens *do not move*. During El Salvador's civil war (1979–1992), approximately one-fifth the population fled into exile – a catastrophic event for the nation by any measure – but that also means the obvious, that four-fifths remained.

To stay or to go? For some, the decision is simple enough: You receive a phone call in the middle of the night, and a sinister voice tells you to get out or else. For most of the others, the process of discernment is much more difficult. In late 1998, I visited Honduras shortly after Hurricane Mitch set the country back decades by washing out 90 percent of its bridges and laying waste to virtually all its arable land. The disaster spawned an exodus of tens of thousands toward the United States. Many of the people I interviewed turned the tables by peppering me with questions about how difficult it was getting across the U.S.-Mexico border and how the American economy was doing; it was clear enough that they were making mental calculations, weighing the risks of leaving or staying. But there were others who, no matter how much they'd suffered, could only imagine a future on their patch of flooded earth.

And where, within these categories, do we place families like Aditi's and Hemant's? Or families like mine? Most of the Angulos have never been refugees or exiles (except for two cousins, one forced to go abroad after a coup d'état in the early 1970s, another during the civil war). And while my grandparents did not follow the letter of the law on their American visas (they were supposed to visit the States every year to keep them current; often, they let two or three years pass, but the immigration officials never denied them entry), they were never considered "illegals." No Angulo had to crawl under a barbed wire fence or get their backs wet by fording the turgid waters of the Rio Grande. Nor did my relatives walk into America through the usual portals, the rough-and-tumble immigrant ghettoes. If they were visiting my family, they arrived in a mostly white and middle-class neighborhood; most of my other relatives established themselves in model suburban comfort.

My family is middle class, and one definition of such status is the ideal and the practice of social mobility, which often means moving in the physical sense: the better job, the nicer neighborhood, the cleaner air are always just over the horizon, the just reward for hard work. Many middle-class citizens of the Third World can imagine these things only beyond the borders of their own country. And yet we usually do not think of the middle class when we think of "immigrants"; by and large we associate the term with the working class. In sheer numbers, middle-class immigrants are decidedly a minority, and it is obvious why. In most of the world, the "middle class" is a tiny social slice surrounded by the vast sector of the working poor and the jobless poor.

The middle-class immigrant leaves the homeland under dramatically different circumstances than his working-class counterpart. The middle-class immigrant usually has "papers" (the most important requisite for an American visa is a healthy bank account). Often, the middle-class immigrant has a well-off relative waiting to receive him in a comfortable home. The middle-class immigrant will often "pass" as a nonimmigrant; he wears American cotton in the form of Levi's and Dockers, the uniform he'd already been wearing in the homeland in emulation of Americana. He will probably not be relegated to "secondary inspection" at ports of entry like his polyester-wearing brethren undoubtedly will.

The middle-class immigrant, above all, believes he has some say in the matter of migration. He believes he is moving because he wants to and because he can, unlike the refugee or the undocumented worker, both of whom often arrive at the moment of departure more out of desperation than desire. And yet this brand of middle-class migrant consciousness is at least partly an illusion, a narrative that masks the fact that the middle class is ultimately as vulnerable to history as any other social group.

Indeed, history often wakes middle-class migrants out of their cosmopolitan reveries. College degrees obtained in the homeland may be worthless in America. And the very American fact of racial consciousness may deny middle-class migrants what they treasure most: their social status. Suddenly, the Pakistani doctor, who enjoyed a kind of privilege in the homeland that would be better compared to the privilege of the American aristocracy, finds that he must work two menial jobs and that raised eyebrows greet him when he looks for an apartment in a mostly white neighborhood.

To go or to stay? What, in the end, determines this fundamental choice? Is it really a choice at all? Is there a genetic predisposition toward migration? Is it a moral issue – from the point of view of those who do the moving as well as those who stay behind – more than a political one? And if it is, where is its canonical text? How to tell if a particular migration is more a running away from something than a running toward? These movements do not occur in a vacuum: for each person that leaves, an entire network of social relations is affected. What redeems the price paid? And what of a society that pays the price millionsfold, through an exodus of refugees, or a brain drain?

Then there are the questions asked by those of us who live in regions that receive the exiles. We wonder, in fear and in loathing, what will happen to "us" as a flood of "them" arrives on our shores: Will the multitude, with their different tongues and gods and mores, build an incomprehensible Babel, tearing the social fabric that holds us together? Will wages be depressed, will the "illegals" take more in public services than they provide with their labor? (A common argument among the anti-immigrant right in America, and yet, by what formula does one calculate the public and private contributions of an undocumented nanny?)

What will happen to the concept of national identity as the sanctity of the nation-state is subverted by the rootless ones?

Many of these questions have no easy answers, and this is somewhat surprising, because so much of what we know of history is the product of human movement. And the history we are writing today is more so than ever a product of that movement, which is occurring on an unparalleled scale. We have had thousands of years to mull it over. Perhaps the problem is that the issue is discussed mostly in the context of political power struggles. To paraphrase the famous dictum, truth is the first casualty of an electoral campaign. The migrant has always been politically vulnerable, a pawn at the mercy of game masters with armies, customs officials, and pliant media at their disposal.

And yet the migrants, working- and middle-class, in all their marginality, have also always been prophetic. They slip through the cracks of political and media spin, confront us, reveal us. The migrants are a mirror in which we see the best and worst of ourselves, our past and our future. They remind us over and again that there is nothing stable in our world: No state, no culture, no religion, no politics is immune from history and the way it shapes space and time.

The migrants tell us that we are, all of us, always on the move.

:: Epilogue ::

IT WAS A SWELTERING AND SMOGGY SUMMER AFTERNOON IN LOS ANGELES, and the circus had come to town in the form of the 2000 Democratic National Convention. Phalanxes of delegates, protestors, and police faced off throughout the four-day event. On more than one occasion, the noxious scent of pepper spray hung in the air and busloads of kids were hauled off to jail. I was covering the convention as a journalist, and I found myself gravitating toward the immigrants. Not the handful of sons and daughters of immigrants that were among the delegates, protesters, and police, but the recently arrived immigrants in whose neighborhoods the convention and "anti-"convention affairs took place, from the Central American barrio of Pico-Union on down through the Mexican areas of downtown near the Staples Center.

Every day, there was a protest march consisting of black-clad anarchists, neo-hippie greens, feminists, anti–prison-industrial-complex and Third World activists, all supporting one another's causes and all vehemently opposed to "globalization"—which to the activists means multinational corporate domination, environmental holocaust, American military adventurism, and neo-colonialism; to sum up, the abuse, on a global scale, of the human right to dignity in labor, a clean environment, and freedom from discrimination on the basis of race, class, gender, sexual orientation, religious affiliation, age, and any other rubric used by human beings to identify themselves or others.

And yet the activists themselves were a product of globalization, too. Since the first anarchist gatherings in the late 1990s at meetings of the World Trade Organization, the International Monetary Fund, and the G-8, their movement had blossomed into an international phenomenon precisely because they've availed themselves of globalization's technologies—particularly the Internet—to spread the word instantaneously around the world and create a virtual organic community. Indeed, many of the activists call theirs the "global justice movement," or claim themselves "alter-globalizationists."

The activist crews would gather at Pershing Square and head off toward the official convention site, ending in a confrontation with the LAPD. The route took them down Figueroa Street for about a mile, straight through the heart of a rough-and-tumble migrant universe of street vendors, ranks of down-on-their-luck recently arrived travelers, sweatshops, taco and pupusa stands, and several *discotecas* blaring out the latest pop hits from south of the border—*narcocorridos* and *cumbia*, *norteño*, rock *en español*, and even rap *en español*. The young activists had dutifully leafleted the neighborhood for several days prior to the beginning of festivities, but, predictably, there were few takers. Many of the denizens of L.A.'s immigrant downtown, sympathetic to the cause or not, wanted nothing to do with the LAPD, which is infamous for acting like a proxy Border Patrol when the streets boil over, as they did during the Rodney King riots of 1992 (when dozens of immigrants—mostly young people—were quietly deported). The operative emotion is fear: fear of contact with any kind of authority figure, lest the immigrants without "papers" lose their fragile hold on their version of the American dream.

During one of the marches, I stopped by a botánica for some shade, and struck up a conversation with an Old World matron who stood behind a display case filled with a plethora of amulets and potions to ward off precisely such evil forces as the Border Patrol and the LAPD. I mentioned to her that many of the activists seemed to want to represent people just like her—hard-working immigrants on the lowest rung of the global economy. "That's very nice," she told me. "But really, do they think that fighting with the police is going to change anything?"

A panting Green on Rollerblades poked his head in the door. "The cops are busting the bicyclists from Santa Cruz!" In a second, he was gone.

The matron shook her head and sighed. "Besides, all this violence is bad for my business—you're my first customer today!"

Later that afternoon, I retreated from the chaos surrounding the Staples Center and headed toward MacArthur Park, the heart of the Pico-Union barrio, remembering those days back in '92 when immigrant grandmothers just like the botánica woman took to the streets and carted off shopping baskets full of Pampers and food as the neighborhood went up in flames. As I approached the barrio, I heard the unmistakable pulse of techno music. Maybe some Salvadoran teens were trying on a new style, I thought to myself.

No, it was a crew of activist youth taking a break from the march and setting up the nightly protest rave. The actual denizens of Pico-Union, who had mostly ceded this corner of the park to the protest ravers for the past several days, began to gather around the makeshift stage, curiously eyeing the new kids on the block. Gradually, the immigrant elders and young couples just off of work, teens in baggy jeans, and tots formed a concentric circle around the neo-tribal white kids from Santa Cruz and Berkeley and points even farther away.

There was a moment when I thought the immigrants would actually join in on the fun. A few of the tots actually pranced about gaily with some of the activists. But most of the immigrants dared not step into the inner circle, no matter how good the will of the ravers to create a multicultural paradise. In the end, the moment was just a sign of possibility, and of how close people were to actually being close in this New America we live in, a country split between "native" and "stranger," between haves and have-nots. A nation ever-veering between an embrace of those whose faces resemble ours least and a slap to that very face.

::

Intense debate swirls around immigration and immigrants. Politicians declaim nativist diatribes that can sway elections—and become public policy. In some ways, the negative representations of immigrants have replaced the bogeymen of the Cold War. But there are pro-immigrant activists in the United States, too. Particularly in faith-based communities and, in recent years, the labor movement, there has been a growing public defense of the immigrant community. At the same time, immigrants and exiles and refugees represent themselves as never before—in popular cinema, literature, music, and yes, even electoral politics.

Indeed, it seems as if two great, contrary narratives are developing simultaneously. One, essentially fundamentalist and exclusionary, is hostile to the migrations that transform our physical and cultural geography. The other is loosely integrationist in the cultural sphere and critiques the enduring economic disparities between the First and the developing worlds (and between "native" and "foreigner" at home).

These conflicting narratives are not unique to the United States. They are as much a part of the global realm as free trade agreements and cultural syncretism. It's no wonder, then, that American nativists seem to share rhetorical if not philosophical ground with Islamic extremists: Both want a return to that mythical time before the fall into global chaos, to retain the "purity" of the culture. It seems that Pat Buchanan and Osama bin Laden actually have a lot in common.

It is obvious that neofundamentalisms—including the recent wave of right-wing populist electoral gains throughout Europe—are a reaction to the changes we witness today. Globalization, in its simplest terms, is a triangle of three interacting forces: the movements of capital, information, and people across the frontiers. The lowering of trade tariffs and the opening of free-trade zones throughout the world facilitate the movement of capital. The technological breakthroughs of the last two decades quicken the flow of information. And the voracious, highly mobile labor economy sends people scurrying from province to city, from east to west and south to north, from Old World to New.

The human element of the globalization model raises the most difficult issues. By and large, the middle classes of the First World are quite happy with the global arrangement when it comes to the mobility of capital and information. The upwardly mobile denizens of newly revitalized American cities enjoy dining in exotic restaurants, dancing to salsa, and listening to world beat on the airwaves (and, perhaps, fattening their stock portfolios with Halliburton shares). They might even directly contract immigrants—legal or illegal—for the most intimate of services, such as nannies for their children. Or erotic massages.

But these same cosmopolitan Americans can, quite without warning, turn on the immigrants, whose very presence has helped to make global culture hip. In cities and towns across America, immigrant and "native" communities shoved together by the economy, legal immigration, and the underground railroad of illegal immigration lock horns over cultural and economic turf.

The 1990s saw small-business lobbies in Los Angeles urge city government to enforce decades-old (and rarely invoked) anti–street vending ordinances against Latin American immigrants proffering mangos, pirated CDs, and used clothes on the sidewalks (unfair competition!). Also in Los Angeles, homeowner associations lobbied to prohibit landscapers (again, mostly Latin American immigrants) from using leaf blowers (noise pollution!). In the Mt. Pleasant district of Washington D.C., yuppies at the vanguard of the recent dramatic re-gentrification of the neighborhood attempted to ban mariachi musicians from performing serenades in public (noise pollution again).

Such disputes have more recently arrived in the American heartland. In the Ozark town of Rogers, Arkansas, local nativists lobbied for, and received, Immigration and Naturalization agents from the federal government to root out the "illegals." Towns in Wisconsin pass "English-only" resolutions; a dozen states have passed or are considering legislation that would make it impossible for undocumented immigrants to acquire driver's licenses. (Two weeks before the unprecedented election that saw his ouster, former California governor Gray Davis signed a bill *allowing* the undocumented to secure driver's licenses; Davis' replacement, Arnold Schwarzenegger, vowed to repeal the law.)

There have also been several cases in which the tensions have led to physical violence. On Long Island, men posing as contractors viciously beat several immigrants who were thumbing for work as day laborers. In San Diego, white teens with guns have been known to take "target practice" on migrants crossing the international line. In Douglas, Arizona, vigilantes armed with assault rifles patrol ranchlands, a tragedy waiting to happen. In a bizarre post-9/11 case in the California high desert community of Lancaster, a Mexican immigrant riding in his car on the freeway was forced off the road and beaten because the assailants thought he was Arabic; but he might actually consider himself lucky. On September 15, 2001, Balbir Singh Sodhi, an Indian-born Sikh, was shot and killed in Phoenix, Arizona, by a man who said he targeted Sodhi "because he was dark-skinned, bearded and wore a turban." According to the ACLU, hate crimes against Arab Americans increased an astonishing 1,600 percent in the wake of 9/11.

::

It is an axiom of modern psychology that we often punish others for traits that are latent in ourselves. What does xenophobic America deny in the immigrant that it denies in itself? Old World ideals of social solidarity that run counter to our "up from the bootstraps" myths? The immigrants' intimate family relations that can seem claustrophobic compared to our own "family values"? Do we misinterpret first-generation immigrant optimism—by all accounts a pillar of Americanism—as a mockery of our narrowing social and economic horizons generations later? Are we embarrassed to admit that the American Dream isn't so dreamy after all? In this light, immigration policy is not just a matter of government spending or assimilation or even about legal or illegal passage across our borders: It is about what we Americans think of ourselves. And it seems as if we don't much like the visage we see in our immigrant-mirror.

As it is in America, so it is across much of the globe.

During France's last presidential election, right-wing candidate Jacques Le Pen railed against the "menace" of North African immigrants and promoted the idea of gathering migrants into "transit camps" before placing them on a train—the deportation special—to England.

Malaysia estimates half a million undocumented workers within its borders; under an "amnesty" program, thousands have recently returned to their home countries (Indonesia, India, Bangladesh), and the government has destroyed their shanties to prevent their return.

Australian Prime Minister John Howard has taken a hard line against Indonesians seeking a better life down under.

Tokyo's police department recently set up a special hotline for citizens to report suspected Chinese migrants, who are associated with crime in the popular imagination.

And on and on: In every corner of the globe, someone from somewhere else is singled out, harassed, legislated against, deported, given the scarlet letter of illegal immigrant status. If W.E.B. DuBois famously and prophetically proclaimed that the divide between white and black would be America's greatest challenge in the twentieth century, it seems as if the very notion of "citizenship"—of who "belongs" and who doesn't within the blurring boundaries between nation-states—will be the world's conundrum for the twenty-first.

::

I was born and raised in California and have, through the better part of my adult life, traveled on a north-south axis, from L.A. to Mexico and Central America and back again. I suppose initially my ideal was to look for my past—my first trips were *Roots*-like odysseys, seeking to reclaim my parents' and grandparents' language and cultures. I soon realized the quixotic nature of my endeavor. There was no way I was ever going to become a Mexican or a Salvadoran, no matter how well I learned the vocabulary and the regional accents: Sooner or later I would always be found out and branded an outsider, the gringo with the luxury of taking such a trip in the first place. The great irony was that as I made my way south, millions of my paisanos were making their way north; I was clearly running against the historical tide. I wanted to learn Spanish, my Latin brethren wanted to learn English; I wanted to claim a past, and they a future.

Ultimately, I decided to follow the migrants northward. Over a period of several years, I tracked the movement of several families from one small town in Western Mexico. Nothing could have prepared me for the destinations I would soon arrive in: North Carolina, Wisconsin, Arkansas, Missouri. I'd known through scattered press reports that some kind of migratory transformation was underway, sending not just Mexicans but Central Americans, Southeast Asians and South Asians, West Africans, and Eastern Europeans not to the typical ports of entry on the east and west coasts, but to the "heartland." I'd read about Hmong refugees arriving in Pennsylvania, about Salvadorans in Dallas, Haitian enclaves in Boston, Mexicans in the cannery towns of Alaska.

One of the reasons that the immigration debate had, long before 9/11, returned to the national agenda was precisely the arrival of migrants to parts of the country that hadn't received "foreigners" for the better part of a century and in some cases much longer. This shock—formerly mostly white, or mostly white-and-black cities and towns receiving strangers from far-flung lands—reignited long dormant discourses and debates. The anti-immigrant fervor of the 1990s may have begun in California, but it resonated on Capitol Hill only because the high-propensity voters of the heartland suddenly felt they had a stake in such matters, too.

But for every citizens' committee holding emergency meetings about what to do about the "furriners," there are other groups, oftentimes communities of faith, and countless individuals who welcome the strangers and urge them on. Talk to the migrants—they'll tell you. About the Episcopal priest who heads out to the steaming tobacco fields in North Carolina on Sundays, offers Mass, hosts a barbecue, and even brings along a whistle to referee migrant soccer matches—the only recreation these men ever have. Or about the big rosy-cheeked Methodist sister who defended the migrants in a small Wisconsin meatpacking town when a vicious, unfounded rumor spread that a Mexican boy had raped a local girl and a lynching seemed a real possibility. There are even Samaritans out on that life-or-death line that the U.S.-Mexico border has become, four-wheeling into the desert in search of migrants in distress.

Most of the media report about vigilante groups arming themselves with assault rifles against the invading hordes (who often cross property lines while trying to elude the Border Patrol). But there are others, like the former New England prep-school teacher whose golden dream of retirement led him to desert paradise in Rio Rico, Arizona. Little did he know that he'd wind up offering food, water, and even his bed to migrants navigating through the searing heat of summer or the brutal, dry cold of desert winter.

Beyond this activist realm, there is a growing space in America in which the immigrant is welcomed and becomes an integral part of a new social fabric. A literal embrace between Others, as it were: Some thirty percent of the newest immigrants—Asians and Latin Americans—marry outside their ethnicity. When I was growing up, being Salvadoran and Mexican was a novelty; these days, whenever I visit a college campus, I'll have students come up to me and say they "identify" with me because they, too, are mixed, in many cases much more mixed than I am. Guatemalan–Iranians. Jewish–Salvadorans. Black–Koreans.

Desire transcending the barriers of race and class is the ultimate affirmation of humanity amid the most dehumanizing aspects of globalization. And therein lies the only hope that I can glean from the darkening horizon at the dawn of the new millennium. A few years ago I led a youth writing workshop in the Mt. Pleasant neighborhood of Washington, D.C., which at the time was a dizzyingly diverse place: Salvadoran, Dominican, and Vietnamese immigrants living alongside African Americans (recent gentrification has diminished this veritable Rainbow Coalition somewhat). It was easy to see the way the newcomers had been influenced by living in what had for decades been a stable, African-American neighborhood: Salvadoran kids were rapping, Dominican kids break dancing, Vietnamese kids wearing baggie jeans and baseball caps backward. But I wondered what, if any, impact the immigrant class had on African Americans. I asked one of the "elders" of the hip-hop generation, a twenty-something freestyle rapper nicknamed "Sweetpea," what he thought.

"Well, I don't think it's the food," he said. "I really don't like the *pupusas*. And it's not the music—can't stand *merengue*.

"But you know, when the *'migos* first came here," he added, using a diminutive of amigos, the African-American term for Latinos in D.C., "I thought about the war in El Salvador and how far they'd come to get here. I guess I realized that the world was a lot bigger place than I thought it was."

For some, the arrival of the Other touches a dark place in the psyche, a place of fear and resentment that surfaces as a refusal to accept any notion of commonality whatsoever. But for people like Sweetpea, the immigrants can inspire notions of solidarity: Sweetpea is an African-American man realizing the commonality of his history and that of his Third World brethren: colonialism and the struggle for liberation.

Ultimately it will be in the everyday relations between people in places like Mt. Pleasant, or a small heartland town, or in the increasingly mixed inner cities across the country, that our future will be determined. And because we see so little of the quotidian interaction between Others represented in the media, it is quite possible that we're much further along in the process of birthing a New America than we think.

::

As the son and grandson of immigrants to America, I have been aware of the distance between "us" and "them" all my life. It is as easy for me to claim American-ness as it is to stand apart from it, an ethnic rebel attempting to foil the melting pot—in just the way that conservatives complain about. I do not claim to speak for all "ethnic rebels," but I can tell you this: When I stand apart, I do so defensively. It is a reaction to feeling that I am being cast as an outsider, for the color of my skin; for where my parents came from; because I speak Spanish as well as English; because I like norteño music in addition to rock 'n' roll; cherish American individualism as much as Old World values of social solidarity. For some, this set of cultural signs is proof of torn allegiances. I may be a secret agent for Mexico's President Fox, I may have plans to re-conquer the Southwest. But if I stand apart from America on occasion, it is not on behalf of Mexico or any other foreign power. It is on behalf of what I believe to be truly American ideals that have been betrayed. America is an exception, but not in the melting-pot sense. It is unique because we are a "nation of many nations," as Whitman once said, "of every hue and caste . . . of every rank and religion . . ."

I have also been aware of a tension between what I choose and what I think has been chosen for me, and I think of this now, as I ponder the lives of the protagonists of *The New Americans*, whose lives seem to be determined to such a great extent by forces beyond their control, by history itself. Americans like to think of themselves as outside of history—or even as the end of it. I wrote my last book in the Mojave Desert. Literary pilgrimage to the desert was clearly my choice, a romantic gesture; a very American, middle-class one—like Henry Miller in Big Sur or Jack Kerouac playing the hobo. But it is more difficult to say that I "choose" to write about the people I generally write about: refugees, exiles, immigrants, "marginal" subjects all. It feels much more like they've chosen me or, perhaps, that history chose them for me. Still, there comes a moment in every writing project when I confront the distance between self and other. I am moved when I ponder Naima Saadeh's extraordinarily painful departure from her homeland—or rather, occupied homeland, which adds tragic poignancy to her leaving, since one cannot really depart from a country that doesn't exist—

because I remember my mother's tears when we'd say good-bye to family at the airport in her native San Salvador. But no, I am not really like Naima Saadeh at all. My American passport privileges me, as does my occupation. I am allowed across the borders between nation-states and beyond police lines. Perhaps I am a bit more like Naima's husband, Hatem, who was born and raised here, his consciousness split between American pop and the traditions—and of course the current political situation—of the Old World.

The media that report the stories of global gypsies contribute to the divide between "us" and "them," of course. From the hometown paper to the local evening news, on up the ladder of audience shares to the voices of ultimate authority like the network broadcasts and *The New York Times*, the distance is actually emphasized because the point of view never shifts away from the "center," i.e., from the media elite themselves and their multinational corporate patrons. The age-old mantra of journalistic "objectivity" reifies what is actually a tremendous "subjectivity": the point of view of a handful of mostly white, mostly male, and, most importantly, all middle- to upper-middle-class people with only superficial contact with their "foreign" subjects. Even the most liberal reporting does not escape this fundamental bias.

I too am a card-carrying member of the American media establishment, inheritor of all its flaws. I can only imagine representing the Other through my subjectivity: searching for common ground, recognizing the differences, admitting my bias, trying to walk in the other's shoes even when I know that it is impossible. I have often thought that the basic liberal media impulse to focus relentlessly on the Other as a method of developing dialogue with the Other is, ultimately, completely backward. After the 1992 Rodney King riots, the proponents of "civic" or "public" journalism, in a fit of liberal guilt over their neglect of marginal communities, placed dozens of camcorders in the hands of the subjects—

most often ghetto teens—that they might document themselves, thereby presumably achieving a more "authentic" representation. But, alas, the raw footage was still edited back at the studio, not in the ghetto. A radical way to begin an equitable dialogue through media imagery might be to have the ghetto dwellers train the cameras on us, the media, the middle class, the political and cultural castes that determine representation in the first place.

Media-as-ideology is nothing new, but American politics once offered at least the possibility of more organic communication among constituencies (which could translate into mass movements). Our democracy today is a virtual phenomenon, a collection of tropes based on mass imagery carefully controlled by political elites and their partners—corporate media outlets that have a tremendous stake in public policy making. Little wonder, then, that "marginal" voices have little control over how they are represented; their agendas almost always run counter to the powers that be. When pro-immigrant activists seek better working conditions and a more open border, their message is turned back by the prevailing ideological winds of big capital, which, of course, opposes any change to the economic system that provides its low-wage, underground workforce.

The exiles of the global realm—the migrants, the refugees, the "illegals," the West's "Others"—are well aware of the fact that today's political battleground is increasingly virtual—and cultural.

::

In the late 1980s and early 1990s, a generation of artists in the American Southwest began to use the border between the U.S. and Mexico—and, by extension, the frontiers not just between nation-states but also the social divides within nation-states—as a metaphor. The border was cast

less as a wall and more as a porous line through which cultural and economic currents constantly flow from one side to the other, creating the
possibility, and often the fact, of a "third space."

The concept of "border culture" gained widespread notoriety thanks
in large part to the media-savvy of the loose collective known as the
Border Arts Workshop/Taller de Arte Fronterizo (BAW-TAF), whose
studio space was literally on the international boundary between San
Diego and Tijuana. One typical BAW-TAF installation was called "Casa
de Cambio," literally, "house of change," which is what Mexicans call
currency-exchange businesses. But at this *casa de cambio*, people were
transformed instead of money: One entered a stereotypical American or
Mexican, and emerged a kitschy blend of both.

Performance and spoken-word artists and rebel academics flocked to
BAW-TAF's kaleidoscopic vision of a world in flux, a post-modern territory where "signs" clashed ceaselessly to create "syncretic" forms like
Spanglish poetry and culinary delights such as the teriyaki burrito. Yet
what was diminished in the concept of border culture as it won a
worldwide audience was the critique of the power relations that had
spawned it. When presented in mainstream venues, the performances
delighted the very kind of public—mostly white and middle class—that
the border artists sought to indict for their complicity in global injustices.
No matter how incisive the political message, it was the kitschy cultural
forms that the well-heeled art patrons identified with and claimed as
their own.

Nevertheless, the early border artists spawned a critical discourse
indispensable to a discussion of the global present. Today the very
notion of "borders" is at the center of much of our experience of the
global realm.

But one's experience of frontiers is determined by one's place in the
cultural, economic, and political matrix. It would seem that the number

of options to position one's self in the world has multiplied, in direct proportion to the apparently increased amount of human movement in search of a different—presumably better—life by crossing the boundaries between nation-states. Ironically, just the opposite seems to be the case. The U.S. boom of the late nineties cleaved the economy in two—the middle and working classes saw little improvement or actually lost ground while the upper-middle's fortunes skyrocketed. To a great degree, wealth followed the contours of the shifting economy: those with connections to the new, hi-tech sectors did well, and those tied to the old industrial economy fared worse. There was one other growth sector: the so-called "service" economy, jobs in which one literally "serves" someone else. Maintenance workers, cooks and busboys, hotel maids, parking-lot attendants, and landscapers. These are almost always non-union jobs that rarely offer even the most basic benefits packages (i.e., health insurance). Even at the height of the boom, the maintenance workers at dot.com companies weren't regaled with stock options. In *The Betrayal of Work*, Beth Shulman notes that some thirty million Americans work full-time and make poverty wages; one in four workers make $18,100 a year or less, placing them at or below the federal poverty line.

If there ever was a global "trickle-down" as a result of the expansion of the U.S. economy and the multinationals, it clearly didn't trickle toward the working poor or jobless poor of the developing world. If anything, the cleaving of the U.S. economy has been replicated worldwide, fattening the traditional ruling classes and leaving the poor, as always, out of luck. What has trickled down, and up, and sideways, is pop culture, the kind that is diffused on the free airwaves and on satellite TV, VCRs, and DVDs.

The popular experience of culture today in many ways resembles BAW-TAF's early performances. The white twenty-something tattoos herself with primitive designs gleaned from a book on ancient Aztec motifs; her boyfriend listens to an Algerian *rai* artist on his Sony Discman. A crew of octogenarian Cuban musicians brought together by a white American blues-guitar player plays Carnegie Hall.

Meanwhile, on the other side of this cultural hall of mirrors, the barrio kid in Mexico City "tags" up subway trains in emulation of New York's legendary graffiti artists. Hip-hop has seized the global youth imagination like rock 'n' roll, and jazz and swing before it.

And somewhere in between, in the "liminal" space as the academics say, there are Mexican *banda* music groups who employ a style of their country's traditional music to perform covers of Creedence Clearwater Revival. Or bands like L.A.'s Ozomatli, an outfit that includes Salvadoran, Mexican, Brazilian, and Japanese musicians who play a mélange of tropical and urban styles, singing in Spanish and English and occasionally dancing the samba. Or my personal favorite, East L.A. legends Los Lobos, who for three decades have made a career out of blending rock, Mexican traditional, country-western, Cajun, and rhythm and blues so well that their sound is impossible to define with any of the usual stylistic markers. Call them cosmic rockers.

For many, this global point of encounter is a thing of beauty. But it is also largely a space of privilege, the realm, ultimately, of the middle class, which consumes these styles as product. Sitting in the audience at Carnegie Hall for the Buena Vista Social Club is a world away, to say the least, from listening to a pirated CD of an old Madonna album on a battered boom box in a Brazilian *favela*. The connoisseurs of World Music like to think of themselves as worldly, that through the grace of art, they commune with their brothers and sisters in far-off lands. But often they do nothing of the sort. The Buena Vista Social Club phenomenon is a case in point. The American and European audiences listen to a beautifully packaged soundtrack that is the equivalent of a time capsule—the music of a time before the Revolution and its successes and failures. It is "uncomplicated" music to the extent that it is completely divorced from the complexities of modern Cuba, absolving the listener from any responsibility in the ongoing crisis of U.S.-Cuba relations.

German art-film director Wim Wender's documentary *The Buena Vista Social Club* captures perfectly the hierarchical relation between the cultural subject and cultural consumer. When the Cuban musicians arrive in New York City for their much-anticipated performance at Carnegie Hall, they are awed by the great symbols of the American empire: the Empire State Building, Rockefeller Plaza, the Statue of Liberty. Cut to a shot of the musicians on stage, the seats of Carnegie filled with the city's elites. There is an uncanny resemblance of these scenes to the stories of "primitive" subjects brought back to the seats of colonial empires to be displayed as if in a zoo.

And what of the Americans or Europeans who listen to Fela Kuti, Nigeria's late "afro-beat" hero? If they read *Fela: The Life and Times of an African Musical Icon*, Yale musicologist Michael Zeal's definitive work, they'd be closer to a close encounter of the global kind. But to listen to Fela without hearing his story—a highly political odyssey under the most repressive regimes imaginable—is like listening to Afro-beat without the percussion tracks.

There is an undercurrent of longing in many of the cultural productions that surface in the global marketplace: the longing for the time before the fall into the chaos of the global era. Even when the production blends Old World tradition with New World pop style, such as in the North African techno-folk of Algerian Rachid Taha, the eclectic rock *en español* of Mexico's Café Tacuba, the jazzy Africana of Mali's Salif Keita or Fela himself (whose funk jams bear the unmistakable influence of American R&B—even as he influenced American musicians like James Brown), the context is everything. A Nigerian in Chicago listening to Fela is listening to his homeland. An American usually imagines only a faraway place of great beats and palm wine.

The world today is divided not just between haves and have-nots, but also between those who must move to survive and those who move because they want to and because they can, between global exiles and globe-trotters. The global exiles are socially positioned on the margins no matter what shore they arrive on. The globe-trotting vacationers are lavishly received by those global subjects who haven't yet made their pilgrimage into exile. The globe-trotters have a great time abroad, while the global exiles sing songs, write poems and novels and essays, produce plays and films, and fill canvases with the metaphors of their never-ending journeys.

::

I'll end where I began: in post-9/11 America. The "nation of immigrants" that, in the two years since the attacks, has detained at least 5,000 foreign nationals on suspicion of terrorist activities. Of these, only five have been criminally charged. Some 6,000 immigrants of Arab descent have been "prioritized" for deportation; tens of thousands more could ultimately be forced out. Is the nation any safer now? The immigrants among us certainly aren't.

The echoes of history ring loudly. In 1919, attorney general A. Mitchell Palmer, in the name of fighting back the "red menace," ordered the detention of thousands of suspected Communists, mostly foreign nationals—among them was feminist-anarchist icon Emma Goldman, who was ultimately deported to Russia. During the Great Depression, nearly half a million Mexicans—a significant number of them actually American citizens—were "voluntarily" repatriated to Mexico. On February 19, 1942, President Roosevelt signed Executive Order 9066, targeting well over 100,000 persons of Japanese descent for relocation to internment camps.

It is obvious enough that immigrants are vulnerable to the designs of hate-mongering politicians: they are "aliens" and do not have the legal recourses that American citizens take for granted. But what, in the end, defines citizenship? I know of a college student who was born in Mexico, crossed into the United States illegally with his parents as a toddler, and has lived here ever since. He graduated with honors from a prestigious university. But by the letter of the law, he remains an "illegal alien." His case is by no means an exception. (Indeed, there are enough such cases that Senator Orrin Hatch and Representative Richard Durbin have sponsored the Development, Relief and Education for Alien Minors (DREAM) Act, which would allow undocumented students to "adjust" their immigration status.)

I know another student. He is an Iraqi national, a doctoral student of anthropology at an Ivy League university. He was forced to register with the government and was questioned by the FBI. He's thinking of moving to Canada.

Is it possible for a society to meet the great challenge—and great contradiction—of e pluribus unum? How does one legislate for the one and the many, create a public policy toward the immigrant that is true both to the nation's highest ideals and the realities of a complex world? In the end, not everyone who espouses immigration restrictions is a nativist crackpot, and not everyone who espouses liberal immigration policy or even open border ideology (a curious political space where libertarian Republicans meet radical lefties) a reckless anarchist. The pendulum-swinging nature of over 200 years of public policy regarding the foreigner is ample evidence that these liberal and restrictionist tendencies represent a tug of war in the American soul.

The problem is that the debate has barely evolved—we are trapped in a static dichotomy. The fact is that our ambivalence about immigration is part and parcel of an even greater contradiction. As Americans we pronounce platitudes about supporting "nation-building" and "fledgling democracies" the world over, when our democracy continues to experience its own growing pains. We have yet to completely overcome our colonial past, our master-slave past, our xenophobic past, but our hubris knows no bounds—with it we construct our militaristic foreign policy and our draconian immigration laws. If America is ever to truly become the exception it claims to be, it must confront the tragic contradiction of being a "raceless" and racist, a "class-less" and classed society. Once again, America must, as it did during the Civil Rights Movement, recognize its failures—the distance between its ideals and its reality. One thing is clear: no matter how much ground the nativist reaction might gain in times of national duress, there is no way to turn back the 200 years of human movement that has shaped our identity. Even if we sealed our borders perfectly, "diversity" would remain a fact of American life. The strangers among us today soon will no longer be strangers. Just as a man named Fiorello La Guardia, the son of Italian and Jewish immigrants, once inspired the city of New York, so today we have the sons and daughters of the new immigrants—who in increasing numbers are taking up positions of leadership within their communities, and beyond them.

In so many ways, our current debate over immigration is a delayed reaction to what has already come to pass. To a certain extent this is understandable. The demographic changes seem to have taken place in the blink of an eye, and in historical terms, they have: during the course of one generation. It's not the first time. Imagine life in New York City at the turn of the twentieth century: the sudden, bewildering encounter between Jews and Irish and Italians and African Americans and the descendants of earlier waves of European migration.

Then, as now, there were those who decried the presence of what Benjamin Franklin once called the "Palatine boors." And such attitudes undoubtedly made what was already a difficult migrant passage into America all the harder for the newcomers. But that generation also received help, from other Americans whose deeds have by and large been forgotten in our shrill immigrant narrative: from school teachers and priests and union organizers, from the occasional politician, from neighbors. This kind of solidarity with the New Americans exists today, in the public life and in the private, as it did a century ago.

Then, as now, we embraced them, we disdained them, we deported them, we married them. It was an awkward, messy, painful, sublime process. It was, it is, an American process.

:: Selected Bibliography ::

Achebe, Chinua. *Things Fall Apart*. New York: Anchor Books, 1994.

Anderson, Benedict. *Imagined Communities: Reflections on the Origin and Spread of Nationalism*. London: Verso, 1991.

Barkan, Elliot Robert. *And Still They Come: Immigrants and American Society 1920 to the 1990s*. Wheeling, IL: Harlan Davidson, 1996.

Bamyeh, Mohammed. *The Ends of Globalization*. Minneapolis: University of Minnesota Press, 2000.

Boahen, A., ed. *UNESCO General History of Africa, Vol. VII: Africa Under Colonial Domination 1880-1935*. Berkeley: University of California Press, 1990.

Chang, Suecheng. *Asian Americans: An Interpretive History*. Boston: Twayne Publishers, 1991.

Darwish, Mahmoud. *The Adam of Two Edens*. Syracuse, NY: Syracuse University Press, 2000.

————. *Unfortunately, It Was Paradise: Selected Poems*. Berkeley: University of California Press, 2003.

————. *Memory for Forgetfulness: August, Beirut, 1982*. Berkeley: University of California Press, 1995.

Davis, Mike. *Magical Urbanism: Latinos Reinvent the U.S. City*. London: Verso, 2000.

Fanon, Frantz. *The Wretched of the Earth*. New York: Grove Press, 1963.

Gilroy, Paul. *The Black Atlantic: Modernity and Double Consciousness*. Cambridge, MA: Harvard University Press, 1993.

Hayden, Tom. *Irish on the Inside: In Search of the Soul of Irish America*. London: Verso, 2001.

Higham, John. *Strangers in the Land*. New York: Atheneum, 1970.

————. *Send These to Me: Immigrants in Urban America*. Baltimore: Johns Hopkins University Press, 1984.

————. *Hanging Together: Unity and Diversity in American Culture*. New Haven, CT: Yale University Press, 2001.

Hirschman, C., J. Dewind, and P. Kasinitz, eds. *The Handbook of International Migration: The American Experience*. New York: Russell Sage Foundation, 1999.

Inda, J.X., and R. Rosaldo, eds. *The Anthropology of Globalization*. Malden, MA: Blackwell Publishers, 2002.

Levitt, Peggy. *The Transnational Villagers*. Berkeley: University of California Press, 2001.

Massey, D., J. Durand, and N. Malone, eds. *Beyond Smoke and Mirrors: Mexican Immigration in an Era of Economic Integration*. New York: Russell Sage Foundation, 2002.

Nehru, Jawaharlal. *Discovery of India*. Oxford: Oxford University Press, 1990.

Pacini-Hernández, Deborah. *Bachata: A Social History of a Dominican Popular Music*. Philadelphia: Temple University Press, 1995.

Quinones, Sam. *True Tales from Another Mexico: The Lynch Mob, the Popsicle Kings, Chalino and the Bronx*. Albuquerque: University of New Mexico Press, 2001.

Rodriguez, Richard. *Brown: The Last Discovery of America*. New York: Penguin USA, 2003.

————. *Days of Obligation: An Argument with My Mexican Father*. New York: Penguin USA, 1993.

Roth, Henry. *Call It Sleep*. New York: Avon, 1973.

Roy, Arundhati. *Power Politics*. Cambridge, MA: South End Press, 2001.

Ruck, Rob. *The Tropic of Baseball: Baseball in the Dominican Republic.* Lincoln: University of Nebraska Press, 1998.

Rushdie, Salman. *Imaginary Homelands: Essays and Criticism 1981–1991.* London: Granta Books, 1991.

Said, Edward. *Reflections on Exile and Other Essays.* Cambridge: Harvard University Press, 2002.

———. *Orientalism.* New York: Random House, 1979.

Saro-Wiwa, Ken. *Sozaboy.* New York: Longman Publishing, 1994.

Soyinka, Wole. *The Man Died: Prison Notes.* New York: Arrow, 1985.

———. *The Open Sore of a Continent: A Personal Narrative of the Nigerian Crisis.* Oxford: Oxford University Press, 1997.

Steinberg, Stephen. *The Ethnic Myth: Race, Ethnicity and Class in America.* Boston: Beacon Press, 1989.

Suárez-Orozco, M., C. Suárez Orozco, and D. Qin-Hilliard, eds. *Interdisciplinary Perspectives on the New Immigration, Vols. 1-6.* New York: Routledge, 2001.

Takaki, Ronald. *Iron Cages: Race and Culture in 19th-Century America.* Oxford: Oxford University Press, 2000.

Veal, Michael E. *Fela: The Life of an African Musical Icon.* Philadelphia: Temple University Press, 2000.

Wald, Elijah. *Narcocorrido: A Journey into the Music of Drugs, Guns, and Guerrillas.* New York: Rayo, 2002.

Wiwa, Ken. *In the Shadow of a Saint.* South Royalton: Steerforth Press, 2001.